D1125104

Miracle
MAINTENANCE

Miracle
MAINTENANCE

Joan
HUNTER

WHITAKER
HOUSE

Unless otherwise indicated, all Scripture quotations are taken from the *New King James Version*, © 1979, 1980, 1982, 1984 by Thomas Nelson, Inc. Used by permission. All rights reserved. Scripture quotations marked (kjv) are taken from the King James Version of the Holy Bible. Scripture quotations marked (amp) are taken from the *Amplified* Bible, © 1954, 1958, 1962, 1964, 1965, 1987 by The Lockman Foundation. Used by permission. (www.Lockman.org). Scripture quotations marked (msg) are taken from *The Message: The Bible in Contemporary Language* by Eugene H. Peterson, © 1993, 1994, 1995, 1996, 2000, 2001, 2002. Used by permission of NavPress Publishing Group. All rights reserved. Scripture quotations marked (nasb) are from the *New American Standard Bible*®, nasb®, © 1960, 1962, 1963, 1968, 1971, 1972, 1973, 1975, 1977, 1988 by The Lockman Foundation. Used by permission. (www.Lockman.org). Scripture quotations marked (niv) are taken from the *Holy Bible, New International Version*®, niv®, © 1973, 1978, 1984 by the International Bible Society. Used by permission of Zondervan. All rights reserved. The Scripture quotation marked (nirv) is taken from the *Holy Bible, New International Reader's Version*®, nirv®, © 1996, 1998 by Biblica. All rights reserved throughout the world. Used by permission of Biblica. Scripture quotations marked (nlt) are taken from the *Holy Bible, New Living Translation*, © 1996, 2004, 2007. Used by permission of Tyndale House Publishers, Inc., Carol Stream, Illinois 60188. All rights reserved. The Scripture quotation marked (tlb) is taken from *The Living Bible*, © 1971. Used by permission of Tyndale House Publishers, Inc., Wheaton, Illinois 60189. All rights reserved.

Boldface type in the Scripture quotations indicates the author's emphasis.

MIRACLE MAINTENANCE:
How to Receive and Keep God's Blessings

Joan Hunter Ministries
P.O. Box 777
Pinehurst, TX 77362-0777
www.joanhunter.org

ISBN: 978-1-60374-941-1
eBook ISBN: 978-1-60374-942-8
Printed in the United States of America
© 2013 by Joan Hunter Ministries

Whitaker House
1030 Hunt Valley Circle
New Kensington, PA 15068
www.whitakerhouse.com

Library of Congress Cataloging-in-Publication Data (Pending)

No part of this book may be reproduced or transmitted in any form or by any means, electronic or mechanical—including photocopying, recording, or by any information storage and retrieval system—without permission in writing from the publisher. Please direct your inquiries to permissionseditor@whitakerhouse.com.

1 2 3 4 5 6 7 8 9 10 11   **ᴜᴜ**   20 19 18 17 16 15 14 13

DEDICATION

This book is dedicated to those who have been healed and will be healed by reading this book. It is also dedicated to those who have lost their healing for some reason and who, through reading this book, will reclaim it and walk out their complete healing.

ACKNOWLEDGMENTS

I would like to acknowledge Naida Johnson Trott, RN, CWS, FCCWS, for all of her hard work in helping me compile all the information in this book, and for her years of devotion to me and my parents, Charles and Frances Hunter.

A special thank-you to my husband, Kelley M. Murrell, for helping edit and update the parts of this book that were adapted from my parents' book *How to Receive and Maintain a Healing.* Thanks for all your help proofing the manuscript and double-checking it for scriptural soundness.

CONTENTS

Part III: Removing Hindrances to Receiving

Part IV: Conditions for Maintaining

INTRODUCTION:

RECEIVING AND MAINTAINING YOUR MIRACLE

Picture a young couple making preparations for the birth of their first baby—a precious gift from God. Clothing, blankets, a crib, food, and a special place are meticulously prepared for the big event. A special doctor is found, and medical advice followed. When the baby arrives, it is not left alone to fend for itself; no, the parents nurture that life with food, love, warmth, and guidance. They praise God for the miracle of their newborn child, and they maintain that miracle by keeping the baby fed, clothed, and protected; having the baby immunized against various diseases; attending to the spiritual upbringing of the baby; and whatever else is needed to care for that child in the years to come.

Your miracle is no different. What have you received? Healing of your body? Miraculous financial provision? Restoration of your relationships? Whatever it may be, you have a responsibility to hang on to it and care for it properly. If you take it for granted, forgetting what God has done, you will likely forfeit that miracle.

In many cases, a miracle from God is not just for the person receiving it; it is meant to be a powerful tool of evangelism for those who witness the miracle.

Again, with everything you "receive," there is a responsibility to "maintain," or you will lose the blessing of that gift. It will become a burden as your time and money and energy are spent, until you wonder if you were blessed or cursed by what you received.

For example, accepting ownership of a house implies your commitment to its upkeep—cutting the grass and maintaining the yard; keeping it freshly painted; attending to repairs; cleaning (or hiring a cleaning service); paying the utility bills; making your monthly mortgage payments; and handling any other issues that may come up. Have you developed the knowledge and funds to manage home ownership?

You must learn the keys to not only maintaining your miracle but how to share it with others. In many cases, a miracle from God is not just for the person receiving it; it is meant to be a powerful tool of evangelism for those who witness the miracle. How are you going to use these tools for the kingdom? These questions are important to ask yourself in your quest to be a good steward of the gifts God gives to you.

Many years ago, my parents, healing evangelists Charles and Frances Hunter, wrote a book entitled *How to Receive and Maintain a Healing*. Many of the principles and revelations they shared are included in this book; however, there is so much more that the body of Christ needs to know in the areas of receiving and maintaining. We will discuss healing of the body, but when you reach the final page, I sincerely hope you will understand that the miracles you receive extend far beyond your physical body to such areas as your emotions, your finances, your relationships, your career, and more.

By the final page of this book, you will have learned to crawl, stand, walk, and even soar into the life God has planned for you, His child. You have the choice to walk into all that God has for you.

> *"For I know the plans I have for you," declares the* LORD, *"plans to prosper you and not to harm you, plans to give you hope and a future."*
> (Jeremiah 29:11 NIV)

Am I teaching you something brand-new? Not at all. Everything I teach is directly from God's Word. I believe that God prepared your heart before you even picked up this book. He has sparked an interest within you to learn more about His provision and love. He has birthed a yearning deep down inside you, and this book will begin to answer that longing for knowledge and truth about your Father.

Miracle Maintenance will change your life as you know it. Are you ready?

PART I:

PREPARING TO RECEIVE

1

THE RULES OF EXCHANGE

"Give, and it will be given to you...."
—Luke 6:38

From social situations to business transactions, the exchange of goods, services, information, and more is the basis of human interaction. There are general guidelines governing the majority of exchanges.

The concept of learning to receive may seem unnecessary. However, it is a very important scriptural truth. Life teaches us to "give and take." God teaches us to "gift and receive." *Aren't they the same thing?* you ask. The terms are often used interchangeably, but there is a difference. Let's consult the dictionary for definitions of these words.

+ **Give:** "to present voluntarily and without expecting compensation; to hand to someone; to place in someone's care; to grant (permission, opportunity, etc.) to someone; to impart or communicate; to set forth or show; present; offer; to pay or transfer possession to another in exchange for something; to furnish, provide, or proffer;...to issue; to produce, yield, or afford; to make, do, or perform; to relinquish or sacrifice; to convey or transmit; to assign or allot; to bestow upon...; to award;...to inflict; to pledge...or execute and deliver;...to concede or grant."[1]

+ **Take:** "to get into one's hold or possession by voluntary action; to hold, grasp, or grip; to get into one's hands, possession, control, etc., by force or artifice; to seize or capture; to catch or get."[2]

+ To me, *taking* implies a negative function. It is not stealing, but close to it in principle.

+ **Gift:** "something given voluntarily without payment in return, as to show favor toward someone, honor an occasion, or make a gesture of assistance; present; the act of giving; something bestowed or acquired without any particular effort by the recipient or without its being earned; a special ability or capacity; natural endowment; talent."[3]

+ **Receive:** "to take or acquire (something given, offered, or transmitted); get; to hear or see; to have (a title, for example) bestowed on oneself; to meet with, experience; to have inflicted or imposed on oneself; to bear the weight or force of; support;...to take in, hold, or contain; to admit; to greet or welcome; to perceive or acquire mentally; to regard

1. give. Dictionary.com. *Dictionary.com Unabridged.* Random House, Inc. http://dictionary.reference.com/browse/give (accessed: June 04, 2013).
2. take. Ibid. http://dictionary.reference.com/browse/take (accessed: June 04, 2013).
3. gift. Dictionary.com. *Dictionary.com Unabridged.* Random House, Inc. http://dictionary.reference.com/browse/gift (accessed: June 04, 2013).

with approval or disapproval; to listen to and acknowledge formally and authoritatively."[4]

What does this have to do with maintaining your miracles? There are boundless gifts for you to receive. Even though you may think of a "gift" as a pretty package wrapped up with ribbon, gifts are not always tangible. Things like respect, honor, favor, and opportunity are also gifts. Compassion, love, forgiveness, recognition, information, instruction, and talents are also gifts to give or receive. A gift can be something as simple as a smile. Regardless of their packaging, gifts are coming at you every day. How do you "open" or receive them? And what is your responsibility once you have done so? Do you take them for granted? Do you set them on a shelf to admire, only to forget all about them? Do you maintain them? Do they add to or detract from your quality of life?

The Rules of Receiving

In most cases, everything you receive comes with conditions attached. What do I mean? Well, let's imagine you win a car. Sounds great, right? However, to claim this gift, there are some conditions you must meet. You must: (1) have a valid driver's license, (2) be healthy enough, mentally and physically, to handle a car, (3) have a garage or other safe place to park the car, (4) be able to afford car insurance, (5) be able to afford the taxes, (6) be able to afford the regular maintenance required to validate the warranty, and (7) be able to afford fuel to power the car. (Pray it gets good gas mileage).

Recently, a young couple "won" a fabulous condominium at a popular vacation spot. It's free; the "only" costs to them will be: (1) insurance, (2) monthly condominium fees, (3) transportation back and forth from their home (1,200 miles away), and (4) property and income taxes. Chances are, they will have to sell the condominium because of these costs that accompany their "free" gift.

Even if you are not "receiving" but "earning" or "purchasing" something, you have to follow the rules. If you find yourself in need of food, you go to the

---

4. *The American Heritage® Dictionary of the English Language*, Fourth Edition, © 2000 by Houghton Mifflin Company. Updated in 2009. Published by Houghton Mifflin Company. All rights reserved.

Even if you are not "receiving" but "earning" or "purchasing" something, you have to follow the rules.

grocery store, select what you want, pay for your purchases, place them in bags/boxes, carry those to your car, drive back home, unload the groceries, put them away, prepare the items needed for your meal, and finally eat.

If you don't want to prepare dinner at home, you may decide to go out to eat—at a restaurant with its own set of rules. You must wear proper clothing, sit at the table indicated by the hostess, give the wait staff your order and wait for the food to be served. Once you have eaten, you pay for your meal, including a tip for the server, if applicable, before heading home again.

Your entire life is truly dependent on others. If you want something, you must pay the price at the proper place and time. One hiccup in the path between creator and consumer means you won't get what you desire.

Yet many people seem to believe they can make it on their own, without any help from anybody else. They are determined to figure out the answers to their problems by themselves. They search the encyclopedia for information and attend one more self-help seminar. They won't admit their dependence on anyone; they work long hours to earn whatever they need. They forget that even in a vacuum—even if they were the only person on the planet—there's still Someone they depend on for survival.

Your Ultimate Provider

God is the Author of everything. Every experience, every emotion, every thought—every breath—is a gift from God. Without a father, a child cannot be formed or born. Your heavenly Father planned your birth, your life, and your destiny. Because of His love for you, you are a co-heir with His Son, Jesus Christ, set to inherit all that God has: His wealth, His salvation, and His eternal life. Because you are the apple of His eye, you can stand in His presence every day, every minute, every second of your life, and know you are blessed.

Do you recognize where your provision comes from? Do you put your faith in your job or your spouse? Do you believe you have to work for every penny? Or do you recognize that every breath you breathe, every penny you earn, is truly a gift from God? Do you take things for granted, or do you offer the praise of thanksgiving to the One who provides? Understanding where things come from and who the true Provider is takes some education. But correct knowledge will save your soul—literally.

One may believe receiving is easy. But is it really? Do you deserve to be healed? Do you believe God wants you to prosper in all things? Or are you operating with the mind-set that God is teaching you a lesson? Do you really think that He wants you poor and sick?

He planned your birth. He knew you before you took your first breath. Think about it—out of the millions of sperm from your father and a specific egg from your mother, God chose the exact match that He wanted to create the unique person you see in the mirror each morning. He knew what talents to place within you, as well as the characteristics you would need in order to thrive. Our Father is a big, big God. He was busy giving you traits and attributes as you were being formed in your mother's womb. He gave you your first breath, your first cry. You were a blessed gift from God to your parents, and your parents, in turn, were a special gift He chose specifically for you.

Our Father created the earth as a gift for all His children to enjoy. Unfortunately, some of His kids are rebellious and destructive instead of being appreciative.

Our Father created the earth as a gift for all His children to enjoy. Unfortunately, some of His kids are rebellious and destructive instead of being appreciative. One day, they too will acknowledge God as Father and bow their knees to Him. However, you and I aren't responsible for anyone's actions except our own.

Are you grateful for every day? Are you thanking and praising your Father for everything He has given you? If you aren't today, you will be by the end of this book.

Learning to Receive

Christians often believe they know exactly when and how God is going to provide for their needs. In these cases, God usually comes from the opposite direction and thoroughly surprises them. I'm not discounting the value of prayer or the importance of searching the Scriptures for precious verses to hang on to. Even believing those precious promises in His Word has a "receiving" component to it. Yet many must learn how to go beyond standing on His promises and actually *receive* them.

This truth comes across in Paul's letter to the Romans:

If you're a hard worker and do a good job, you deserve your pay; we don't call your wages a gift. But if you see that the job is too big for you, that it's something only God can do, and you trust him to do it—you could never do it for yourself no matter how hard and long you worked—well, that trusting-him-to-do-it is what gets you set right with God, by God. Sheer gift.
(Romans 4:4–5 MSG)

When someone tries to bless you because God has prompted him or her to do so, what is your reaction? Do you cross your arms over your chest or hide them behind your back and say, "Oh, no, I don't really need this"? Or do you thank the person politely, giving God all the glory?

Money doesn't grow on trees or drop out of the sky, yet you ought to expect His provision to come from equally unexpected sources. His gifts will be channeled through other people. You should anticipate His blessings around every corner. He can use anyone at any time to bless you as an answer to your prayers. Open your heart to receive them. Open your hands to reach out and take hold of them.

A friend of mine, who was in a desperate situation of her own, tried to give me a sacrificial gift. My first impulse was to say, "No, you need this more than I do!" She turned to me and firmly said, "No, you will accept this gift. You won't rob me of my blessing." I smiled, agreed, and willingly received what she had in her hand.

And still, I had to learn to say, "Thank you!" What makes the difference? Now, I know what will happen when you freely "give" God a gift. He freely and abundantly blesses those who give joyfully with a grateful heart.

Personally, I had to learn how to receive. Now I am teaching others how to do the same. For years, I felt unworthy to receive anything I hadn't worked hard to obtain. It says in 2 Thessalonians 3:10, *"If anyone will not work, neither shall he eat."* This led me to believe that I didn't deserve anything unless I labored for it or somehow earned the money to purchase it. Yes, I "received" pay for my work; however, I felt that I "deserved" that pay because I had "earned" the money through my efforts. I accepted nothing unless I had worked for it; I felt unworthy to receive free gifts. Even though I had been a Christian since the age of twelve and had always recognized God as my heavenly Father and Source of everything, I still had to learn to receive. I had to look in the mirror and practice saying, "Thank you very much." It may sound ridiculous, but it's true.

Your life depends on the ability to receive—and the ability to maintain what you have received. Reading this book will show you exactly how. It will transform your life because this information will affect every area of your life. You will change the way you think. You will love with a new heart. You will see with renewed sight. And you will live with the heartbeat of God.

2

THE GIVER OF
ALL GOOD THINGS

*"If you then, being evil, know how to give good gifts to your children,
how much more will your Father who is in heaven give
good things to those who ask Him!"*
—Matthew 7:11

*"Every good gift and every perfect gift is from above,
and comes down from the Father of lights,
with whom there is no variation or shadow of turning."*
—James 1:17

Years ago, I heard someone tell an interesting story to explain God's provision, and I would like to share it with you. What if your earthly father put an unlimited amount of money in a checking account just for you, and all you had to do is write a check to access that money and purchase anything you desired? Wouldn't you take advantage of that provision?

Well, our heavenly Father has a warehouse of blessings for each of His children, just waiting for them to draw from and enjoy. His bank account is overflowing, and He has given you the password to open it and receive all He has stored for your use and enjoyment.

Everything you have received, and everything you will receive in the future, is a gift from Him. You can never earn His unconditional love or do enough to be truly worthy of His bountiful blessings. He wants you to have a good life, so He explains what you need to do and pursue, as well as things to avoid, which are detrimental to your existence and may block His blessings from reaching you. The only condition is that you are one of God's children, for only those who call Him Father are qualified to receive His blessings.

Are You a Child of God?

For as many as are led by the Spirit of God, these are sons of God. For you…received the Spirit of adoption by whom we cry out, "Abba, Father." The Spirit Himself bears witness with our spirit that we are children of God, and if children, then heirs; heirs of God and joint heirs with Christ, if indeed we suffer with Him, that we may also be glorified together.
(Romans 8:14–17)

Again, all people are created by our Father God and receive from Him daily. However, to receive God's best, you must recognize Him for who He is and also receive His Son as Lord and Savior. In other words, your first experience of "receiving" from God occurs when you open the door to your heart and allow Jesus to come in. Along with His presence and eternal salvation, you receive His Holy Spirit to lead and guide you—and so much more.

If you have never taken this step, I invite you to pray with me and accept Jesus Christ into your heart as the Lord and Savior of your life.

Father, I recognize You as the Creator and Source of all good things. I know that in order to be considered worthy to receive Your best for my life, I must accept Jesus, Your Son, as my Savior. Forgive me, Father, for the wrong things I have done in the past. I know I can't be perfect, but I am willing to give my life to You, and I ask Jesus to come into my heart. I believe that He died so that I could be reconciled to You, and I believe that He rose from the dead so that I might receive eternal life. I do not want to be separated from You any longer; I want to be born again into a new life with You. Please send Your Holy Spirit to guide me and teach me as I seek to follow You from this day forward. Thank You, Jesus. It is in Your name that I pray, amen.

The Benefits of Being God's Child

When you are born again into God's kingdom, not only do you receive salvation and the right to be called His child; you become entitled to receive all of God's promises. In order to do that, you need to know what they are! That's one reason why it's important to read the Bible—it's a blueprint of the countless blessings that rightfully belong to each and every child of God. When you realize what you are entitled to receive as a child of the King, you can experience heaven on earth. You have been adopted as the son or daughter of the God of the universe, and He wants to bless you and heal you!

Salvation

If you confess with your mouth the Lord Jesus and believe in your heart that God has raised Him from the dead, you will be saved. For with the heart one believes unto righteousness, and with the mouth confession is made unto salvation. (Romans 10:9–10)

Only through the blood of Jesus can any man ever hope to enter God's holy presence. Jesus made the way.

Saved or unsaved, no human can ever qualify to enter God's presence. Man is inherently sinful and will always be that way. Only through the blood of Jesus can any man ever hope to enter God's holy presence. Jesus made the way. When you opened the door of your heart and let Him in, He opened the door to heaven for you to enter. No one will ever be good enough, but your big Brother, Jesus, gives you a free pass into an eternity with Him.

The Bible says in Romans 10:17, *"So then faith comes by hearing, and hearing by the word of God."* In simpler terms, to keep faith working successfully, you have to continue reading, speaking, and listening to the Word of God. So, we will continue using His Word as the Source for principles leading to success in both receiving and maintaining the wonderful blessings He gives to us.

The Indwelling Holy Spirit

And I will pray the Father, and He will give you another Helper, that He may abide with you forever. (John 14:16)

[Jesus said,] "It is to your advantage that I go away; for if I do not go away, the Helper ["Comforter" KJV—the Holy Spirit] will not come to you; but if I depart, I will send Him to you....When He, the Spirit of truth, has come, He will guide you into all truth." (John 16:7, 13)

But you shall receive power when the Holy Spirit has come upon you. (Acts 1:8 KJV)

When Jesus gave His final instructions to His faithful followers, He told them to wait until they were endued with power. What kind of power was He talking about, and why did the disciples need it? He was talking about the Holy Spirit, the third member of the Godhead, who lives within every believer.

Jesus had experienced the hardships and struggles of life. He knew that mankind would have a difficult time walking in victory over the enemy without supernatural assistance. Even Jesus needed the help of the Holy Spirit, on more than one occasion, during His years on earth. However, He had to return to heaven before He could ask His Father to send the Comforter to help the believers on earth.

Often neglected or ignored, the Holy Spirit seems to be the silent partner of the Trinity. However, the Holy Spirit brings power from heaven to live within you forever. This is not a simple or insignificant event! What does the Holy Spirit do? Why is the "Comforter" important?

> *Often neglected or ignored, the Holy Spirit seems to be the silent partner of the Trinity. However, the Holy Spirit brings power from heaven to live within you forever.*

To answer these questions, it is helpful to consider some other names for the Holy Spirit: *"Counselor, Helper, Intercessor, Advocate, Strengthener, and Standby...the Spirit of Truth"* (John 14:16–17 AMP). The Holy Spirit is your constant companion—the part of the Godhead who is always by your side, guiding you and strengthening you through life's journey. He can tell you whether you should stop, move, turn around, flee, or continue forward in your present path. His warnings can save your life. In contrast, He can tell you much about the people you meet.

Wouldn't you like a Best Friend forever to walk with you and talk with you whenever you wanted or needed Him? Wouldn't you welcome Someone who would give you the perfect advice in every situation of life? Computers may be a source of endless information; however, the Holy Spirit knows everything—especially what is best for the particular situation you face right now. Supernatural wisdom and understanding are available at any moment. Don't resist all He wants to give you. Open your heart and receive this immeasurably great gift of God.

Now we have not received the spirit [that belongs to] the world, but the [Holy] Spirit Who is from God, [given to us] that we might realize and comprehend and appreciate the gifts [of divine favor and blessing so freely and lavishly] bestowed on us by God. (1 Corinthians 2:12 AMP)

The Fruit of the Spirit

But the fruit of the Spirit is love, joy, peace, longsuffering, kindness, goodness, faithfulness, gentleness, self-control. (Galatians 5:22–23)

A person may say he is saved, but if he continues in his old habits birthed in the enemy's camp, the change is not authentic. If there is a true heart change, there will be an outward change, as well. Part of the change that happens is that he begins to exhibit what the Bible calls the fruit of the Spirit. Instead of being mean, selfish, ugly, and hateful (attributes of Satan), suddenly, he undergoes a personality change and begins to express joy, kindness, gentleness, and love (attributes of Jesus).

For you were once darkness, but now you are light in the Lord. Walk as children of light (for the fruit of the Spirit is in all goodness, righteousness, and truth), finding out what is acceptable to the Lord.
(Ephesians 5:8–10 NKJV)

When you are saved and filled with the Holy Spirit, your entire life changes. Some people undergo a transformation so profound, no one can recognize them. For others, the change happens gradually. No matter the timetable, when you accept God as Father, your lifeblood changes from evil to good. The Holy Spirit's infilling changes your spiritual DNA.

Spiritual Gifts

There are diversities of gifts, but the same Spirit. There are differences of ministries, but the same Lord. And there are diversities of activities, but it is the same God who works all in all. But the manifestation of the Spirit is given to each one for the profit of all: for to one is given the word of wisdom..., to another the word of knowledge..., to another faith..., to another gifts of healings..., to another the working of miracles, to another prophecy, to another discerning of spirits, to another different kinds of tongues, to another the interpretation of tongues. But one and the same Spirit works all these things, distributing to each one individually as He wills. (1 Corinthians 12:4–11)

Not only do you receive the Person of the Holy Spirit into your life, He comes with gifts. Best of all, He chooses specific giftings just for you. Many of them may be shared in common by several other people; however, He knows which ones you need for the challenge you are facing.

As each of you has received a gift (a particular spiritual talent, a gracious divine endowment), employ it for one another as [befits] good trustees of God's many-sided grace [faithful stewards of the extremely diverse powers and gifts granted to Christians by unmerited favor]. (1 Peter 4:10 AMP)

Like anything else, you must receive these gifts and maintain them. The more you use the gifts of the Spirit, the more comfortable you become with them. And these gifts are to be shared, not stored or hoarded. Often, they are meant as tools for witnessing to others.

One of the spiritual gifts is discernment. There is nothing weird or eerie about it; however, you may suddenly feel an urgency to move, to leave the present environment or avoid a particular person. This discernment is God's Holy Spirit warning you of the enemy's presence. You have heard of "women's intuition." This is God's intuition, in the form of the Holy Spirit speaking directly to your spirit. Pay attention to the nudges of the Holy Spirit when He reveals something about a particular situation.

Fresh Insights

The Scriptures say that when Paul, formerly known as Saul, came to saving faith, his eyes were opened, and *"something like scales"* fell from them. (See Acts 9:18.). Following salvation, reading the Bible becomes a totally new experience.

Jesus described this special insight to His disciples in the following way:

You've been given insight into God's kingdom. You know how it works. Not everybody has this gift, this insight; it hasn't been given to them.

Whenever someone has a ready heart for this, the insights and under-
standings flow freely. But if there is no readiness, any trace of receptivity
soon disappears. (Matthew 13:11–12 MSG)

You may have read a certain verse dozens of times, but when you read it
again through believing eyes, you begin to understand it in a different light,
as the Holy Spirit illumines God's Word in new ways. There is a dawning of
comprehension as you "receive" fresh revelation. God gives you this understanding—what a wonderful gift!

Countless Blessings

When you are born again, you become God's favorite. You are now His
child, and you have an open invitation to approach His throne. He is your
Father—your Source for all things. You have become worthy to receive all
God's blessings. Along with His salvation, He gives you the key to your own
storeroom of endless supply. You are in His family, and that fact alone grants
you access.

He offers His protection, His wisdom, His provision, His love, His Son,
and His Spirit freely to all of His children. If you are His child, then when
you accept His contract (His Word), obey His rules, and agree to work His
garden—the earth—you will reap a bountiful harvest.

Faith to Receive

All things are possible to him who believes. (Mark 9:23)

Another gift you receive by the study of God's Word is the faith to
receive your miracles from Him. Yes, we all have been disappointed. Many
people doubt miracles are real or believe miracles will happen for them. Yet
you are surrounded by the miraculous at every moment. When you rou-
tinely read the Bible, you learn to recognize the hand of God in every situation, thereby affirming your belief that He is the Giver of all good things
and your trust that He will prove faithful in taking care of you every day.

As in everything else, you have to make a choice. You have to choose to
believe that you are healed and blessed by the hand of almighty God; that

you are free to walk in the wonderful plans He has for your future. Then, when the enemy tries to torment you with doubt and lies, you can laugh in his face and shake off the symptoms of pain, hurt, sin, and the burdens of yesteryear. You will act out what you believe.

Many people doubt miracles are real or believe miracles will happen for them. Yet you are surrounded by the miraculous at every moment.

I have met many people who "know" something to be true, yet they believe something different. Jesus gave believers His authority to overcome the enemy and to heal diseases:

Then [Jesus] called His twelve disciples together and gave them power and authority over all demons, and to cure diseases. (Luke 9:1)

[Jesus said,] "Behold, I give you the authority to trample on serpents and scorpions, and over all the power of the enemy, and nothing shall by any means hurt you." (Luke 10:19)

Do you really believe that all of these promises are absolutely true for every single area of your life? When you have experienced hurt, abuse, and brokenness, you may find it difficult to believe that these truths are for you. Cling to them and apply them in every area of your life. You are no longer a victim of the enemy. You are an overcomer by the blood of the Lamb and the word of your testimony. (See Revelation 12:11.)

Choose to Believe

When you have come to believe in Christ and have accepted Him as Lord and Savior, it is time to start acting on your belief. Right now, choose to believe that every truth in Scripture was written for you, personally. Find just one thing that you know is a true miracle of God. Write it down. Next, look for another and another and another. Write down every one of them. Soon you won't have time to write down every blessing that is being poured over you. Then, when you find yourself in need of a little faith-boosting exercise, get out your list of blessings and read them aloud, praising Jesus for every one of them. Soon, your mood will lift, and you will be adding even more blessings to your list.

> *Then your light shall break forth like the morning, your healing shall spring forth speedily, and your righteousness shall go before you; the glory of the LORD shall be your rear guard. The LORD will guide you continually, and satisfy your soul in drought, and strengthen your bones; you shall be like a watered garden, and like a spring of water, whose waters do not fail. Those from among you shall build the old waste places; you shall raise up the foundations of many generations; and you shall be called the Repairer of the Breach, The Restorer of Streets to Dwell In.* (Isaiah 58:8, 11–12)

God's Word is truth. You can trust Him to supply your every need, to protect you from harm, and to bless you *"exceedingly abundantly above all that* [you] *ask or think"* (Ephesians 3:20).

A Lifetime Guarantee

Many of the material goods you purchase come with a warranty or guarantee of some sort. That way, if something goes wrong or the item proves defective, you may return it to the manufacturer for a full refund or replacement. Before making a significant purchase, perhaps you like to research the reputation of the manufacturer and to check online reviews of the product, so that you can make your purchase with confidence. You want the best, after all. If something breaks down during the first week of ownership, you will get upset and question the quality or worthiness of the object.

Let's do some research right now. What do you know about the Source of all things? How reliable is He? What is His reputation? We're going to search the "reviews"—the Scriptures, as well as real-life testimonies from modern-day people—for proof of what Jesus has done and is doing, that we might know what to expect from Him. Of course, you should expect the unexpected, because God is sovereign; He acts according to His agenda, not yours. But the process of familiarizing yourself with His proven track record from the past will build your faith for what He will do for you in the future.

Are you ready? Let's begin by considering some of the earliest accounts of the wonders of God manifested in the lives of His children.

3

JESUS' MIRACLES THEN

"They cried out to the LORD in their trouble,
and He delivered them out of their distresses."
—Psalm 107:6

Jesus is the ultimate Healer and Miracle Worker. He prescribes a cure for every ailment, and He is handing yours to you right now. But maybe you aren't sure you can trust Him. Maybe you doubt His qualifications. That's why we are about to look at the track record of the ultimate Healer and Miracle Worker of all time, studying thirty-seven of His miracles, as recorded in the Gospels: Matthew, Mark, Luke, and John.

Not all of the miracles we are about to discuss concern healing. Yet each miracle of Jesus is a demonstration of His power over some principle allowed into the human race through the fall of Adam. As a whole, they demonstrate His control over nature, Satan, disease, pain, and death. Bury the truth of these miracles deep within your spirit, until you know that you know that *"with God all things are possible"* (Matthew 19:26; Mark 10:27). The more that you can get them in your spirit, the easier it will be for you to not only receive but also maintain your miracle, because maintaining a miracle requires as much faith as receiving the miracle in the first place.

A Sampling of Miracles

As we examine the following miracles of Jesus in the New Testament, keep in mind that these are only a sampling of the wonders that Jesus did. The gospel of John suggests that many miracles were not recorded:

> *And truly Jesus did many other signs in the presence of His disciples, which are not written in this book; but these are written that you may believe that Jesus is the Christ, the Son of God, and that believing you may have life in His name.* (John 20:30–31)

> *And there are also many other things that Jesus did, which if they were written one by one, I suppose that even the world itself could not contain the books that would be written. Amen.* (John 21:25)

Again, the Bible records only a select few of the numerous miracles Jesus actually performed. From a study of the biblical record, you can learn all that you need to know in order to minister like He did, producing healings and other miracles.

There are many things you need to watch for as you read these thirty-seven miracles. Read every Scripture verse carefully from your preferred version of the Bible. Don't just skim over them, assuming you know what they say. Allow these verses to speak to you in a new and different way. You will notice that many of them contain a silent cry of desperation.

With each summary, I will offer a few words of wisdom and application.

Miracle No. 1: Jesus turned water into wine at the wedding in Cana. (John 2:1–11)

Perhaps the most significant part of this account is when Jesus' mother, Mary, said to the servants, *"Whatever He says to you, do it"* (John 2:5). Those words apply to us today, as much as they did to those to whom they were originally spoken. Whatever Jesus tells you to do, you should do without question. Don't be disturbed by what He asks; just do it, regardless of whether it makes sense to you in the natural. Obeying Jesus is the wisest way to live! We will discuss this further in a later chapter.

Miracle No. 2: Jesus healed the son of a nobleman. (John 4:46–53)

Jesus healed the son of a nobleman from Capernaum—and from a distance. When the son was miraculously saved from death, God got the glory. As a result, the man's entire household believed. What a witness!

This miracle demonstrates what faith can do. It simply says, *"So the man believed the word that Jesus spoke to him, and he went his way"* (John 4:50). The man did not question Jesus. He simply took Him at His word. He did not say, "Keep praying for me!" He simply believed what Jesus had said to him.

Faith makes miracles a reality! Jesus saw the man's faith, not just his desire. In John 4:48, Jesus spoke frankly when He said, *"Unless you people see signs and wonders, you will by no means believe."* He understood that many people follow signs and wonders; when, in actuality, signs and wonders should follow those who believe.

Miracle No. 3: Jesus became invisible. (Luke 4:28–30)

Jesus was able to walk through a crowd without anybody seeing Him. This means either that He became invisible or that everyone was blinded to

His presence. Sounds pretty unbelievable, right? Yet nothing is impossible with God if you believe. His miracles come in many forms and in so many ways. He knows the perfect time and the ideal way to bring Himself glory through every miracle.

Miracle No.4: God abundantly supplied a great catch of fish. (Luke 5:1–11)

A fisherman named Simon was very tired after fishing all night with nothing to show for it. When Jesus told him to throw his nets into the deep, Simon did not want to follow His instructions. But he obeyed nonetheless, saying, *"At Your word I will let down the net"* (Luke 5:5). And God blessed him with a catch so great that the fisherman's net began to break and his boat began to sink. (See Luke 5:6–7.)

This miracle illustrates God's provision in all things. He did not give just enough; He gave more than enough. He abundantly supplied when Simon had positioned himself in the correct place to receive. In a later chapter, we will talk further about the proper positioning to receive divine provision.

Miracle No. 5: Jesus drove demons from a possessed man. (Mark 1:23–27; Luke 4:33–36)

Jesus did not waste time talking to the devil all night long. He did not argue with an unclean spirit. Knowing the demons had to obey His authority, Jesus merely told them to come out of the man. There was absolutely no question in His mind as to who He was. The people were astonished when they saw His authority—the same authority He has granted to you.

> *Most assuredly, I say to you, he who believes in Me, the works that I do he will do also; and greater works than these he will do, because I go to My Father.* (John 14:12)

When you use the name of Jesus and speak with His authority, any unclean spirits will come out, exactly as they did when Jesus spoke those words. Many sicknesses, including cancer, may be caused by demonic spirits.

Christians and sinners alike are attacked by cancer-causing demons. In these cases, the only cure comes by casting out the demonic spirit in the powerful name of Jesus.

Several years ago, my parents were conducting a meeting where a woman asked my mother if she had ever known anyone who was healed of epilepsy. A young man standing nearby spoke up and said, "May I answer that question for Frances?" She agreed, and he continued, "She laid hands on me nine years ago and cast out the spirit of epilepsy, and I have never had a seizure since that time!"

The only requirement for the laying on of hands and the casting out of demons is knowing the power in Jesus' name when addressing the demon(s). No shouting is necessary, nor should you argue back and forth with the devil. The demonic spirit simply must leave at the name of Jesus!

Miracle No. 6: Jesus healed Simon's mother-in-law. (Luke 4:38–39; Matthew 8:14–15; Mark 1:30–31)

This story is so simple, it's summed up in a matter of just two verses in each of the three gospel accounts where it appears. It was a simple gesture or touch on Jesus' part that brought the miracle to pass. If you can believe that Jesus still reaches down and touches lives today, that's all it takes—just a tiny spark of faith is enough to make a miracle occur in your life.

The miraculous healing of Simon's mother-in-law happened as any everyday occurrence in Jesus' life. He came to visit and found a family member ill. Without fuss, He just reached out and touched her, and she was healed in an instant. Immediately she arose and assumed her duties as hostess.

Every day, you have the opportunity to reach out and touch those whose paths intersect with yours. How many people do you come into contact with on an average day? The number is probably higher than you would have guessed. And each life is an opportunity for you to share the gospel, to pray, and to speak healing. Allow Jesus living in you to work through you to heal others. Be on the lookout every day for someone who needs a word from Him, and be open to receive that word, that you might deliver it faithfully to a heart in need of healing or encouragement.

Miracle No. 7: Jesus cast out demons and healed all the sick. (Matthew 8:16–17; Mark 1:32–34; Luke 4:40–41)

It is exciting to see people healed with one touch of the power of God. Jesus had thousands at His meetings, and He prayed for them on His own, in solitary times with His heavenly Father. In the years that have passed, Jesus has not changed. His desire is to heal "all," just as He did then—and He wants to do it through you.

Jesus ministered to large crowds, day after day. When the size of a crowd exceeds our abilities, we must find other ways to minister to them, such as training healing teams to minister. Jesus works through His children who follow Him obediently by laying hands on and praying for others.

Jesus ministered to the people so easily and quietly. I believe that's the way He wants you to do it on an everyday basis. In cases where a person is prayed for but not healed, it is often because the person praying has complicated the gospel message instead of keeping it as simple as it was two thousand years ago.

If you find yourself in need of healing, know that Jesus wants to heal you today, exactly the way He healed all those who were diseased in His day. He wants to heal all who are sick. It's a simple process. Don't struggle, strain, or sweat to receive your healing. Just relax and keep your eyes on Him! He made it simple, and He expects you to keep it that way.

Miracle No. 8: Jesus healed a man with leprosy. (Matthew 8:2–4; Mark 1:40–44; Luke 5:12–15)

In all three accounts of this healing, Jesus affirms His willingness to heal. It is the will of God to heal you. It is His will that you be whole and remain whole. Before the leper asked Jesus to heal him, he fell down and worshipped Him—the One with the power, authority, and desire to make him whole.

Jesus is saying, "From the bottom of My heart, with all that I am, I want to heal you. I don't want to see you in a sickbed! I want you to stay well. I want to satisfy your deepest longings. I delight in giving you the very desires of your heart." (See Psalm 37:4.)

Jesus wants to heal you just as much as you want to be healed. You don't need to beg or plead with Him. He is holding His arms out to you, saying, "I want to heal you." That is His desire. It isn't His will for you to be sick! So, be open to accept His free gift of total healing.

Miracle No. 9: Jesus healed a man of paralysis. (Matthew 9:2–8; Mark 2:3–12; Luke 5:18–26)

Jesus healed a paralyzed man whom his friends had lowered into a room through an opening in the roof. All three accounts point out that Jesus *"saw their faith"* (Matthew 9:2; Mark 2:5; Luke 5:20). His focus was on the faith they had acted on—their determination to get their friend to the Master Healer, no matter what—rather than on the ailment of the paralytic. Faith is more powerful than frailty!

Romans 4:17 says that God *"gives life to the dead and **calls those things which do not exist as though they did**."* As important as it is to speak in faith, God needs to "see" your faith in action, not just hear you say what you believe. Jesus *"saw"* the faith of these men, proven by the extreme lengths to which they were willing to go to help their friend.

Miracle No. 10: Jesus healed a lame man by the Pool of Bethesda. (John 5:2–16)

To the sick man at the Pool of Bethesda, Jesus said, *"Do you want to be made well?"* (John 5:6). A few sentences later, He simply said, *"Rise, take up your bed and walk"* (John 5:8).

Not only do you need to know that Jesus wants to heal you; you must want to be healed. You need to determine that you absolutely want to be healed. Whether it's a big sickness or a little illness, you must want to recover!

Illness can be a convenient way to get out of work, school, or church—an excuse not to do something else. The man at the pool brought up an excuse not to get healed. He had a negative attitude. He told Jesus, *"Sir, I have no man to put me into the pool when the water is stirred up; but while I am coming, another steps down before me"* (John 5:7). Some people soak up the extra attention they receive while they are sick—yet this is detrimental to healing! Look for your healing, not for excuses or sympathy.

Miracle No. 11: Jesus healed a man with a withered hand. (Matthew 12:10–13; Mark 3:1–5; Luke 6:6–10)

The Pharisees in this scenario questioned Jesus' decision to heal someone on the Sabbath because they did not want the man to receive his healing. I love how Jesus answered them in Matthew 12:12: *"Of how much more value then is a man than a sheep? Therefore it is lawful to do good on the Sabbath."* Jesus told the man, *"Stretch out your hand"* (Matthew 12:13; Mark 3:5; Luke 6:10), and the man was instantly healed, overriding the Pharisees' spirit of legalism.

Miracle No. 12: By a spoken word, Jesus healed the dying servant of a centurion. (Matthew 8:5–10; Luke 7:2–10)

Jesus healed the centurion's dying servant by sending His word. Jesus then commended the great faith of the centurion. Prayers do travel over long distances. You don't have to be in the immediate vicinity of the person for whom you are praying in order for your prayers to be effective. Ministering on television, online, over the phone, and so forth works just as well. How often has the anointing of God traveled the airwaves through TV or radio to the other side of the world and healed the sick or ministered salvation to the lost? God knows no barriers such as miles or time. No matter the method, God's word of healing works when it is spoken in truth.

Miracle No. 13: Jesus raised a young man from the dead. (Luke 7:11–15)

Jesus had such compassion on this mother, who had lost her only son. He did not speak to the mother; He spoke to the young man, and he sat up immediately, having been made alive and well again! Jesus gave life to the dead.

There are many people in our world who are physically alive yet spiritually dead. Your words, spoken in faith, can raise them from spiritual death. Share your testimony and spread the gospel!

Miracle No. 14: Jesus healed a man who was demon-possessed, blind, and mute. (Matthew 12:22–23; Luke 11:14)

Jesus healed a man who was demon-possessed, blind, and mute. Afterward, the man both spoke and saw. Jesus is the name above all names. He had and He has all power at His fingertips. Through us, His power can still be manifested in the world today.

Healing is something we should expect to happen. The Bible doesn't devote fifty pages to one healing. It merely states that the people brought Him one who was possessed with a demon, and He cast the demon out. Scripture doesn't say a thing about the faith of the person involved. When Jesus spoke the word, the devil came out! And the same thing is possible today. If you believe that Jesus lives inside of you, you can speak His name, with the result that demons flee. Jesus is speaking to you today. What do you need? He has the answer.

Miracle No. 15: Jesus calmed the sea. (Matthew 8:23–27; Mark 4:35–41; Luke 8:22–25)

The disciples' reaction at the tumult of the sea is the picture of panic. They had trusted Jesus and followed Him onto the ship, but when the storm came up, the wind nearly blew their faith away.

When Jesus stilled the stormy tempest, His disciples marveled that the winds and the sea obeyed Him. They didn't realize that everything in the universe is subject to the name and voice of the Creator of the world.

Miracle No. 16: Jesus cast out the demons from the Gadarene man, and he was healed. (Matthew 8:28–32; Mark 5:1–13; Luke 8:26–33)

Jesus didn't specialize in just one type of miracle. He was capable of doing any and all kinds of miracles, and He is still capable today, if you only remember that *"Jesus Christ is the same yesterday, today, and forever"* (Hebrews 13:8).

In this account, Jesus cast the demons out of a possessed man living in the tombs in the country of the Gadarenes. The healed man then fell to his knees and worshipped Him.

> *Jesus sent him* [the man whom He had delivered from demons] *away, saying, "Return to your own house, and tell what great things God has done for you." And he went his way and proclaimed throughout the whole city what great things Jesus had done for him.* (Luke 8:38–39)

Miracle No. 17: Jesus healed a woman who had suffered twelve years with an issue of blood. (Matthew 9:20–22; Mark 5:25–34; Luke 8:43–48)

Because of her tremendous faith, the woman with the issue of blood was totally healed when she touched the hem of Jesus' garment. And He said to her, "*Daughter, be of good cheer; your faith has made you well. Go in peace*" (Mark 5:24; Luke 8:48; see also Matthew 9:22).

It is also significant that Jesus noticed power going out of Him. There were hundreds of people around Him, brushing up against Him; yet He remarked, "*Somebody touched Me, for I perceived power going out from Me*" (Luke 8:46). Even with so many other people touching Him, He did not feel power going out of Him until this woman touched His garment. No one else was looking for healing with her determination. Her faith drew power out of Jesus to the extent that He felt it.

Miracle No. 18: Jesus raised a young girl from the dead. (Matthew 9:18–19, 23–26; Mark 5:22–24; 35–43; Luke 8:41–42, 49–56)

This account tells of a miracle within a miracle. If you will recall, miracle no. 17 was the healing of the woman with an issue of blood, which interrupted the miracle of the raising of Jairus's daughter from the dead. In all three gospel accounts of this event, the healing of the woman with an issue of blood interrupts the story of the miraculous resurrection of Jairus's daughter.

It is not uncommon for me, while laying hands on the sick, to be directed by the Spirit of God to go lay hands on someone else, instead. An interruption or delay in one person's miracle becomes the instant in which God works a miracle for someone else.

Miracle No. 19: Jesus restored the sight of two blind men. (Matthew 9:27–31)

A mere five verses in one gospel account are devoted to the healing of two blind men. Consider what happens today when a blind person gets healed! I rejoice without ceasing.

Notice that these two men were blind in both eyes. Jesus simply touched their eyes and said, *"According to your faith let it be to you"* (Matthew 9:29), and they were healed! Let your faith develop and grow as you read about these miracles. According to your faith, you will be healed!

Miracle No. 20: Jesus healed a mute man of demon possession. (Matthew 9:32–33)

There are several unique aspects of this passage of Scripture. Some people brought a mute, demon-possessed man to Jesus, and He cast the devil out. This detail is implied, however, for it says, *"When the demon was cast out…"* (Matthew 9:33). It doesn't say that Jesus fought with the devil for hours and hours. It doesn't say that He "prayed" the demon out. Jesus simply chose the correct words, spoke with authority, and cast the devil out.

Miracle No. 21: Jesus fed five thousand people with only five loaves of bread and two fish. (Matthew 14:15–21; Mark 6:35–44; Luke 9:12–17; John 6:5–13)

There is no question that feeding the five thousand was a miracle. God demonstrated His provision and ability to multiply in an unlimited measure. Even if you should be one of five thousand sick and hungry, God always has provision for you. He knows about you, even though there may be millions of others who are also sick. He provides what you need, whether it's healing or resources or something else, no matter what your circumstances happen to be at the time. There is always enough healing power for everyone. If you will note, there was more food left over after the feeding of the five thousand than there was before. That's God's compassion! That's God's provision! That's God's love!

Miracle No. 22: Jesus walked on water, and so did Peter. (Matthew 14:22–33; Mark 6:47–51; John 6:16–21)

This story is full of miracles to remember in times of sickness or other hardship. First, Jesus walked on the water. Second, Peter walked on the water. Third, Peter began to sink. Fourth, Jesus brought him into the boat, and immediately they were on the land!

Apply this story to your needs. There are times when you will be required to walk on stormy seas with all the faith you can find. Those times will stretch your faith like never before. If you need a healing, or if you have received a healing but are still questioning God, remember Peter. With his eyes on the Master, he was doing what was impossible—walking on water. When he put his eyes on his circumstances, he lost what he had gained by faith. When the miracle was over, the disciples found themselves immediately on shore. Consider this—if your condition starts to worsen, cry out to Jesus; He will reach down and touch you, and immediately you will be healed!

Keep your eyes on Jesus and obey His voice alone. Don't react to your surroundings but maintain your focus on the Master. That's how you experience His miracles.

Miracle No. 23: Jesus healed a Canaanite woman's daughter of demon possession. (Matthew 15:21–28; Mark 7:25–30)

This mother was persistent. She didn't give up. She knew Jesus had the answer to her most desperate need—the deliverance of her daughter from demon possession. She admitted that her need was far beyond anything she could accomplish in the natural. Jesus did not answer her immediately, but she was persistent, and He took notice, granting her the desire of her heart. You need to persist in believing in faith until you receive the miracle you need. Never give up!

Another detail worth noting about this account is that the woman worshipped Jesus. (See Matthew 15:25.) She recognized His authority and expressed her gratitude from a thankful heart, and Jesus rewarded her.

Miracle No. 24: Jesus restored healing to a man and healed him of a speech impediment. (Mark 7:32–37)

This man did not come to Jesus by himself; he was brought to Him by some friends. When your faith wavers, the faith of your believing friends can be a tremendous help in your receiving a healing. Gather together with others who believe in healing. Surround yourself with faith, and yours will grow! Jesus heals in many ways, and sometimes He will use a friend to get you where you need to be, whether physically or spiritually.

Miracle No. 25: Jesus fed four thousand with seven loaves and a few small fish. (Matthew 15:32–38; Mark 8:1–9)

The disciples were doubtful of Jesus' ability to feed the masses of people who had gathered there that day, but Jesus defied their skepticism. You may have family members or friends who will speak nothing but doom and gloom concerning your healing. If so, you must remember that you and God are the majority. Don't allow the pessimism of others to deflate your faith!

Miracle No. 26: Jesus healed a blind man of Bethsaida. (Mark 8:22–26)

Again, we see a blind man being brought by his friends to Jesus. And it is the friends, not the blind man, who ask for his healing! Jesus touched the man once, but it was not until He had touched him a second time that his healing was complete. Therefore, you should never be ashamed to go back more than once for your healing. Doing so shows not a lack of faith but rather persistence to receive a full manifestation of healing.

Miracle No. 27: Jesus healed a man's son of demon possession. (Matthew 17:14–21; Mark 9:17–29; Luke 9:38–43)

The disciples had tried to cast the demon out of the child, to no avail. Then Jesus stepped in and rebuked the unclean spirit. When they questioned Him as to why they had failed, He replied,

Because of your unbelief; for assuredly, I say to you, if you have faith as a mustard seed, you will say to this mountain, "Move from here to there," and it will move; and nothing will be impossible for you.

(Matthew 17:20)

He narrowed down the issue even further, adding, "*However, this kind does not go out except by prayer and fasting*" (Matthew 17:21). His response illustrates both the need for faith and the role of spiritual discipline in your walk with God. You must believe in the release of His power, but you cannot neglect your secret life with Him, either.

Miracle No. 28: Jesus paid His taxes with provision from a fish. (Matthew 17:24–27)

How many fish swim around with money in their mouth? Not many, and yet the very first fish Peter caught was the one Jesus had been expecting! Peter found a coin that was the exact amount needed to pay the required government taxes. Jesus can meet your need in any number of ways, from any number of sources. Just be obedient to Him and expect your miracle! And never tell me God doesn't have a sense of humor.

Miracle No. 29: Jesus healed a blind beggar using mud. (John 9:1–7)

An important key to this man's healing was his obedience to Jesus when He told him to go and wash in the pool of Siloam. He did just what Jesus said, and he came back seeing. However, there were skeptics present—just as there are today—who questioned how it had been done. They didn't believe Jesus could perform such miracles, and they questioned the timing of the apparent miracle, for He performed it on the Sabbath—a time when such a thing was considered unlawful. (See John 9:16, 19, 24, 26.) The beggar stood strong and replied, "*If this Man were not from God, He could do nothing*" (John 9:33). He gave a wonderful discourse on the power of God to heal, and it is worth studying. (See John 9:30–33.)

Miracle No. 30: Jesus healed a woman who had been bent by a spirit of infirmity for eighteen years. (Luke 13:11–13)

This woman apparently had arthritis or osteoporosis. She had been bent over for eighteen years. When Jesus spoke to her, she was instantly made whole and began to glorify God. The rulers of the synagogue were again upset with Jesus because He healed on the Sabbath day. (See Luke 13:14.)

Miracle No. 31: Jesus healed a man of fluid retention. (Luke 14:1–6)

Dropsy is a condition in which an excess of fluid causes extreme swelling somewhere in the body. A cause could have been serious heart failure or lymphedema (excessive fluid trapped in the arms or legs, which is also called elephantiasis).

Jesus ministered to the man, healed him, and let him go. (See Luke 14:4.) This miracle doesn't tell how the fluid left the man's body, but it is further proof that nothing is impossible with God! (See Matthew 19:26; Mark 10:27; Luke 1:37.) It was a miracle they could see—an instant healing.

Miracle No. 32: Jesus healed ten lepers. (Luke 17:11–19)

This story opens with a cry of desperation from ten men. Jesus instructed them to test their faith; He said, "Go, *show yourselves to the priests*" (Luke 17:14). As they turned to go, they were not yet healed. If they had gone to see the priests while still showing signs of their disease, not only would they have looked foolish; they also would have been punished. But "*as they went, they were cleansed*" (Luke 17:14). The actual healing occurred as they went, walking in faith to see the priests. They had to put their faith in action in order to receive their miraculous healing.

Oddly, only one of the men who had been healed of leprosy returned to express gratitude to Jesus. We are told that he "*fell on his face at His feet, giving Him thanks*" (Luke 17:16). His "heart of thanksgiving" was poured out at Jesus' feet. At his heartfelt expression of gratitude, Jesus told him, "*Your faith has made you well*" (Luke 17:19). His body was restored to health.

Miracle No. 33: Jesus raised Lazarus from the dead. (John 11:1–44)

> [Jesus] *said to them* [His disciples], *"Our friend Lazarus sleeps, but I go that I may wake him up." Then His disciples said, "Lord, if he sleeps he will get well." However, Jesus spoke of his death, but they thought that He was speaking about taking rest in sleep. Then Jesus said to them plainly, "Lazarus is dead. And I am glad for your sakes that I was not there, that you may believe."* (John 11:11–15)

Jesus spoke in faith about a miracle He was going to see in the future. He referred to Lazarus as sleeping, even though, in earthly terms, Lazarus was dead. Jesus turned a bad situation into a good one. He used this event to build the faith of His followers. When He reached the tomb of his friend, He reminded them of His previous teaching.

> *Jesus said…, "Did I not say to you that if you would believe you would see the glory of God?"…And Jesus lifted up His eyes and said, "Father, I thank You that You have heard Me. And I know that You always hear Me, but because of the people who are standing by I said this, that they may believe that You sent Me."* (John 11:40–42)

Jesus was demonstrating His communication with His Father in front of the people. He didn't take the credit for the miracle; He gave the glory to His Father. He was witnessing to His friends in order to increase their faith.

Jesus said to them, *"Loose him, and let him go"* (Luke 11:44). But He didn't go to Lazarus right away. No, Jesus waited two days after hearing of Lazarus' death to go to him. Lazarus' sister Mary chastised Jesus for His delay, saying, *"Lord, if You had been here, my brother would not have died"* (John 11:32).

We tend to be impatient—we want our healing, and we want it now! But Jesus demonstrated that He heals in His perfect timing. It amazes me how He ministered healing easily and without fanfare. He did His part—praying to the Father—and then He involved the witnesses, asking them to take away the stone and loosen Lazarus' grave clothes. You can do the same today. Jesus living in you prays, and you can lay hands on the sick to release His healing power and minister freedom from the "grave clothes" of the world.

Mary had faith that Lazarus would not have died if Jesus had been there, and she knew he would be raised in the resurrection. Yet she didn't have the faith for a "now" miracle. In the same way, countless people today believe that Jesus can heal; they just don't believe He will heal now, today. They hang on to the assurance that they will go to heaven when they die, but they limit this hope to their eternal destiny, never imagining the blessings available to them now, in this lifetime. Maybe you are among them. Believe for your miracle today!

Miracle No. 34: Jesus healed blind Bartimaeus. (Mark 10:46–52; Luke 18:35–43)

Blind Bartimaeus was persistent. In spite of the crowd, he was determined to reach the Son of David. He recognized Jesus' authority and knew exactly what to do. He knew what he wanted Jesus to do for him. He was specific.

When Bartimaeus heard that Jesus was coming his way, he cried out. He begged for mercy, in a show of repentance. When he learned that Jesus was calling him, *"throwing aside his garment, he rose and came to Jesus"* (Mark 10:50). God answers whenever any of His children calls out for mercy. He responds when His kids ask for a specific healing or a miracle. When you approach God's throne with a petition and present it boldly, He will respond.

This story demonstrates an act of faith by this blind man. Jesus spoke the word of healing, and *"immediately [Bartimaeus] received his sight, and followed Him, glorifying God. And all the people, when they saw it, gave praise to God"* (Luke 18:43) Bartimaeus didn't run away and hide. He immediately followed Jesus, gave glory to God, and publically announced his miracle to others. Soon other people joined him in giving God the glory!

You can never give God too much praise. He deserves all the praise and all the glory from all men, for all eternity.

Miracle No. 35: Jesus cursed a fig tree, and it withered immediately. (Matthew 21:18–22; Mark 11:12–14, 20–26)

Every miracle that Jesus did reminds me that absolutely nothing is impossible with God, if we will only believe. Jesus cursed the fig tree to demonstrate not that miracles *can* happen but that they *do* and *will* happen. This is one of the most important things to remember in receiving a healing. His name is above and over all.

Miracle No. 36: Jesus restored the ear of a man after it had been cut off. (Luke 22:49–51; John 18:10)

When the crowd came to the garden of Gethsemane to arrest Jesus, Peter drew a sword, attacked the servant of the high priest, and cut off his right ear. Immediately, Jesus *"touched his ear and healed him"* (Luke 22:51). In spite of the tense situation, Jesus kept His calm and was a witness to God's power and glory by healing someone who would have been considered His enemy. This is one more instance to prove that nothing is impossible with God, even to the restoration of something that has been cut off. He has the best "glue" of anyone I know. Jesus was also concerned for those who were not believers.

Miracle No. 37: Jesus brought about a miraculous catch of fish. (John 21:1–14)

The disciples were instructed to move the boat a few feet to bring in a great catch of fish—not a logical instruction, but a miracle-producing instruction nonetheless. The disciples weren't even aware that the directions were coming from Jesus, their Friend, because they had seen Him crucified, dead, and buried. They were not yet aware that He had resurrected.

This story supports our discussion on positioning yourself to receive from God. If you are open and obedient, He will reveal to you where you need to be to receive His best.

In actuality, this event was two miracles in one. Yes, catching the multitude of fish was a miracle. But consider this: Jesus appeared to His friends after his death. Jesus then prepared breakfast for the men from their great catch of fish. Can you imagine the King of Kings cooking a meal over a fire on the beach for you? He has actually prepared a feast for you in His Word. You can partake of it anytime you want—on the beach, in church, in your secret place. His food is available 24/7. As you catch fish (people) in the world (sea), bring them to Jesus (on the beach). His Word (the Bible) will feed them.

As long as you are positioned spiritually to receive, your feast is prepared and ready. Yes, even today, the miracles of Jesus are available to you. Don't believe me? Read on—I think you will change your mind.

4

JESUS' MIRACLES TODAY

"He who did not spare His own Son, but delivered Him up for us all,
how shall He not with Him also freely give us all things?"
—Romans 8:32

One of the most important aspects of receiving and maintaining a
miracle is to know that *"Jesus Christ is the same yesterday, today,*

and forever" (Hebrews 13:8). You must believe that what He did yesterday, He will do today and will continue doing tomorrow! We surveyed thirty-seven specific miracles reported in the Gospels. However, to merely accept and believe them with your mind is not sufficient. Until God gives you fresh revelation and insight into these miracles, the words remain only as information, nothing more. Once you receive that spiritual understanding from God, they will come alive inside you.

Some Christian scholars believe and teach that the miracles of Jesus were isolated events limited to the time of the biblical record. However, this belief contradicts the truth of Hebrews 13:8. I believe that His miracles have been as active every day since the very first miracle He performed—turning water into wine at the wedding in Cana. (See John 2:1–11.)

The problem is not that His miracles have ceased but that we have failed to recognize His workings in the world. But by the time you finish this book, you will know without a doubt that God's powerful hand of blessing is at work all around you, pouring out miracle after miracle.

Is Jesus still busy working among His people? Oh, yes. Miracles happen everywhere. They are not reserved for the church or for those in church leadership. And if Jesus lives in you, then you can pray and see the same results, no matter where you are. Whether we are flying across the country in a jet plane, in a submarine at the bottom of the ocean, or in the thickest jungle on earth, God hears our prayers and pours out blessings in response. People are healed of all kinds of issues—emotional, physical, mental, financial, and so on—throughout the earth. His blessings will find His children, wherever they are.

> *The sick in Third World countries believe their only hope is Jesus and in desperation, they reach out to Him. He responds by healing them!*

Many people ask me why it seems easier for people in Third World countries to be healed than in the United States. We see the same miracles and healings in our services, no matter what part of the world we minister in. However, it is true that in the Western world we always have an "alternative" solution. We have hospitals, Medicare, pills and other modern remedies that are not available overseas. The sick in Third World countries believe their only hope is Jesus and in desperation, they reach out to Him. He responds by healing them! They also do not tend to be shy about sharing their miracles with others.

Our ministry office receives hundreds of testimonies every month of miracles from around the world. Only a few will be included here, because we see hundreds every week, during most meetings, and it would be impossible to record every one. Some of these miracles occurred immediately, while others took more time to manifest. But one truth is proven by all of them: Everyone who seeks, finds. Everyone who knocks gains access through the "door" to the blessings of God. (See Matthew 7:7–8; Luke 11:9.) Freedom and healing are available in every area of life—you need only ask.

Physical Healings

Neck, Spine, and Back

"Thanks to your healing prayer, I'm having a great day because there's no pain in my neck where there was a ruptured disk. I'll always be thankful to you."

—GLB

⌣

A sixty-year-old gentleman came for prayer in Denver, Colorado. Bent over in a contorted posture, he explained, "I have a problem with ten vertebrae." My reply was, "You just need a complete new spine." He agreed. As I started praying, I saw a spine in my peripheral vision. Suddenly, he straightened up into the posture of a young man with a big grin on his face.

⌣

A nineteen-year-old young man came forward at a recent meeting. He explained that he had received a prophecy that he would play football in the NFL after college. He believed the prophecy and had been working out vigorously to get in the best possible physical condition. His one concern was that he needed to be taller to be a serious contender for professional football. I prayed. He grew about four inches. When we were at the end of ministering, his father came down to join his son at the altar, and he was totally amazed. Before prayer, the father had been taller than the son; now, the son was taller than his father.

⟞

A young lady came to me in Ireland. She appeared to be about eight years old and spoke with a little girl voice. She asked for prayer that she could grow. It seemed like an odd request, until she explained a heart condition had stunted her growth. She was actually fifteen years of age. I prayed to restore her growth to normal. Within three to five seconds, she suddenly was six inches taller. Her younger sister jumped up and down beside her, cheering. She opened her eyes and was totally amazed as she exclaimed, "Wow, I'm so tall!" She had been about the size of her eight-year-old sister; now, she was looking down at her younger sibling with joy and excitement.

Hips

"I was scheduled for hip replacement surgery in a week. I hobbled up to the front of the church for prayer and was able to walk back to my seat pain free. I cancelled the surgery!"

—HSGI

Skull

"Thanks for praying for my mom, who fell and fractured her skull. She had to undergo surgery on both sides of her head to remove pressure from the blood. Yesterday it was a miracle how she started to talk. She pulled the feeding tube out and is now beginning to eat again."

—PSI

Teeth

"A member of your prayer team prayed for my niece's teeth. Her dentist asked her who filled the cavity that they had found, and she said, 'No one did!' God had healed her teeth! Thank You, Jesus!"

—BRND

Eyes and Ears

There was a lady who pastored a homeless mission. A seventy-year-old gentleman came to her for ministry. He wanted his eyesight restored. Kelley prayed; nothing happened. He prayed again; nothing happened. Instead of being legally blind, he could see with a blur. The lady didn't give up. She continued to pray. Following the third prayer, the elderly man could see.

⌒

Among the twenty-three people on the JHM healing team in Haiti, God moved to open three blind eyes and three deaf ears. Many reports were shared relative to financial blessings since the last visit of JHM. It was amazing to see the miraculous changes that He had performed since we were last in Haiti. The hungry hearts absorbed the message, put them into practice with faith, and were now reaping the benefits of God's prosperity.

Feet, Ankles, and Legs

"As I continue my focus on the Word of God and speaking it out of my mouth, manifestation of healing is increasing. We went to the store last night. My husband noticed I was picking my feet up. It wasn't a struggle, as it used to be in the past. Before, though I would try with all my might to pick up my right foot, I just couldn't do it. ("'Not by might nor by power, but by My Spirit,' says the LORD"—Zechariah 4:6.) Before I started believing God for my healing, I was at the point of wearing out my right shoe in three days. I walked around the mall this week, yet there is no wearing down of my right shoe. My back is continuing to get stronger."

—DWN

⌒

An Indiana gentleman had bone fragments in his foot from a previous incident. Doctors told him he needed surgery. The date was scheduled, but money to pay for such treatment was not available. He came to Kelley for prayer. The pain left, and the swelling disappeared.

⌒

A lady had crushed her kneecap. She limped her way to the altar to receive prayer. Joan laid hands on the damaged knee and spoke healing to the ligaments, tendons, and bones of the area. Instantly, God replaced the kneecap. Pain was gone. Her limp was gone. She was healed.

⌒

A man came to a service with a unique problem: he had been born without a calf muscle in one of his legs. The afflicted leg was skinny and weak. While Joan prayed for another person's leg, the man looked down and realized his problem leg was now the same size as the other. He flexed his leg and realized he had been healed. No one had laid hands on him. Just being in God's presence had caused the anointing for healing to overflow onto him.

Pancreas

"So many people have been healed through Joan Hunter Ministries. My pancreas was healed just by attending your school of healing, and no one even prayed for me for that!"

—CSA

Disease

"Fifteen years ago, you prayed for my husband, who was diagnosed with hepatitis C. One year from the date, he received the news that he was healed. The doctor even shook his hand and said he had no answer as to why there was no virus—dead or alive—in his body. It has been a wonderful miracle, and he is still hepatitis C free. Thank you for doing what God has called you to do and for the blessings that have been brought forth through your ministry. I do believe that God is actively working in each of our lives today, and all we have to do is ask and have faith that He has answered the prayer of our hearts. God bless your ministry and you."

⌒

"Dear Joan and the incredible team at JHM: I am typing this with a big smile on my face and tears in my eyes. After twenty-three years of illness, my friend has been healed of hepatitis C and advanced cirrhosis of the liver! My husband and I had seen Joan on Sid Roth, watched all the archive shows, and then come to the morning service in October 2012 and class in November 2012. One day after we had attended the class, I stayed after work and prayed for a friend I work with. She had been on the liver transplant list for over a year and was on her fourth experimental drug.

"When I prayed for her, I held her hand and commanded the virus to go and cursed the source of the trauma and commanded a new liver. Later that evening, I got the word from Jesus that 'the virus is gone.' I did not mention this to her but just waited on the Lord. It took a while to get the confirmation in the physical. She had a follow-up appointment and lab tests with the transplant doctors. She came back to report these exact words: 'The virus is gone'!"

—NCOG

⌒

"I read a prayer over my eleven-year-old son, who was diagnosed with sarcoma. I read it every night for months as he went through chemotherapy and prayed on a molecular level about the 125 trillion cells. I commanded them to line up chemically to the perfect RNA and DNA that God created. I said the prayer faithfully over my son, along with other healing Scriptures. After a twelve-hour surgery to remove the tumor, the doctors stated that it was 90 percent dead, and the 10 percent left was not sarcoma. One report said it was benign! They stated they rarely say this, but Matthew is cured!"

—SCP

⌒

"My six-year-old daughter had gotten sick on the weekend, and since my wife and I minister together, one of us had to stay home. I was going to be the one to stay home, but I got ready for church, just like normal. My daughter had a fever and a congested chest. We made plans to watch the service online, via Skype. My daughter sat in my lap as we started to watch the worship service. They started the worship with a song about the God of the angel armies.

"About five minutes into the service, my daughter jumped down from my lap and started running in circles, shouting, 'Daddy, an angel just touched me, and I am healed! It is my first miracle!'

"We went to church, and the worship service was still going on. We got to give a witness for healing and bless the Lord.

"The next week, my wife had a sore throat; she described it as having razor blades in her throat. We prayed with faith, and she woke up completely healed. Glory."

⌒

"Thanks to Jesus Christ, first, and secondly to you who prayed for the lady who was suffering from HIV/AIDS diseases and tuberculosis. The day I sent to you the prayer request, the lady was dying—coughing seriously and manifesting chronic breathing problems—and could not walk. She was carried to our Bible teaching class.

"After your prayers, that same day, the coughing and breathing problems all ceased. Three days later, she went for the medical test again and found she was completely healed. She called me from the hospital to say that she went for a medical test when she realized that she had gained strength. After the test, it was noted by the medical doctors that there was no sign of HIV/AIDS or tuberculosis anywhere in her body.

"She went on to say that the doctors who initially screened her blood twice for HIV and tuberculosis were surprised this time that no sign of sickness was found. She asked me to extend her thanks to you who prayed for her. Her lifestyle of prostitution has changed completely, and she wants to give the rest of her life to serving the Lord, to live for Christ and die for Christ.

"She was to attend a job interview, and the director said they needed her medical reports—this was why she quickly went for the medical test. Happily, she was healed and can now get her job, as well. With God, nothing shall be impossible. The news of the healing is now inviting other sick people to our meetings and Bible classes for prayer."

—Pastor LS, Africa

Fertility and Women's Issues

"In April 2010, we were praying for a baby. At a Joan Hunter conference in Denver, she agreed with us in prayer and prophesied that we would have a child within a year. She also gave us a pair of baby bootees. In May 2010, someone from AMC church prayed for us. We got a word of knowledge that 'the Son of God wants to bless you with a son.' In June 2010, we got pregnant, and in March 2011, our precious son, NJJ, was born. In January 2012, Joan Hunter was back in Denver, and we got to introduce her to the baby she had prophesied to us about. Glory to God!"

—REJC

⌐

"I had three miscarriages prior to [Joan] coming, and she prayed for me to be able to get pregnant within the year, and ten days later…I discovered was pregnant! It is God's wonderful miracle and blessing in our life, and we love to share what He did for us. Blessings!"

⌐

Joan attended a home delivery of a baby. Usually, the mother's bleeding eases off and stops once the placenta is passed. Instead, the woman began to hemorrhage. Joan quickly found her Bible and read healing Scripture after healing Scripture while the midwife considered calling 9-1-1. Joan prayed. The bleeding stopped. Instead of being rushed to the hospital, the new mother stayed home to enjoy her new baby.

⌐

"This is not a story about answered prayer, or wanting a baby, but rather about how God keeps the promises He makes to us.

"In August 2010, my husband and I went to a wedding in BC. One afternoon, while taking our kids to the hotel pool, I had a vision of me carrying a baby girl who looked like my daughter. I told my husband that I was pregnant. He didn't really believe me, so I let it drop. A few weeks later, my pregnancy was confirmed. Unfortunately, at eight weeks, I lost the baby. I was pretty upset, but we felt that we had received a promise from God. We decided to try again. Sadly, in between that October and 2011, we lost two more babies—three altogether.

"After the last one, I was depressed, and we pretty much quit trying. We had two children at home to concentrate on. Move forward to June 2011. We had a ministry come to our church called Joan Hunter Ministries. She had a healing ministry, and I attended one of the evening meetings. I went up for my hearing problem and happened to mention the miscarriages. She prayed for me that I would have a baby within the year. Within a month, I was pregnant.

"It was a pretty frightening time for us, to be honest. I wanted to have complete faith, but I had problems for the first three months and had to be on meds. I had placenta praevia after twenty weeks and was on severe restrictions. Although we always knew she was a girl, and believed in our hearts that she would be safe, we were still afraid. Our human tendency to mistrust God was still there, despite His promise.

"February 5, five weeks early, and by emergency C-section, our wonderful baby girl was born, fighting and healthy. She was on oxygen for the first twenty-four hours, and then had jaundice, but she was a fighter. Even the doctor called her a tiger as he tried to get her to join us—she fought them taking her out, and then again when they tried to give her oxygen.

"God is amazing. She looks like the little girl in my vision, and she will be six months in August. God keeps His promises.

"If He has made a promise to you, hang in there. Believe that He is faithful and just and will do as He has said. We weren't even looking for another little member to our family, but God saw fit to make us a promise, because He had a purpose to fulfill in her life and in ours, for His glory."

Multiple Issues

"Joan, I saw you on Sid Roth's *It's Supernatural!* I had just changed the channel, and you were talking about healing. Before I knew it, you said a prayer about healing people with schizophrenia and depression. I put my hand on my heart and could feel those afflictions leave my body! I have suffered with schizophrenia and depression my entire forty-six years. I am now four weeks free of awful medications….Thank you so much for your gift of healing!"

⌒

"I attended a meeting in Duluth, Minnesota, last year. My mother and I came up for prayer. The team prayed for the trauma in my back/hip and warts on my hands. Since then, I have had no back/hip problems. The warts have all gone away! I don't even have scars from where they used to be! I love looking at my hands now; before, I couldn't stand the sight. Thank You, Jesus!"

—DNA

⌒

A man in Guatemala was very excited about his healing. He came forward seeking and received. Following prayer, he rejoiced for his two new knees. When I called for any men with cancer of the prostate, the man returned to the altar to stand in for his father, who was bedridden with his disease. When he went home to share this incredible experience with his family, he found his father out of bed and doing better. His father reported his strength returned about the same time as the prayers were said at the meeting. His mother needed a new heart. She got one. Miracles for everyone! The man returned to his doctor and received verification. His new knees were doing very well.

⌒

"I ran into a large cactus in my yard. My fingers were filled with the stubs of needles impossible to remove. It was painful and burned every time one finger touched another. During your service, you talked about something as small as a finger, and it rose up in my heart how much Jesus cares about even the little things in our lives—things like fingers filled with cactus needles. In that instant, the needles and the pain in my fingers vanished.

"In 2000, I suffered congestive heart failure and lived with angina and other symptoms of that condition for nine years. In November 2009, Jesus healed my heart of what two doctors and a heart specialist had said was an 'incurable' disease. Jesus not only healed my heart; He healed my entire body, from the crown of my head to the soles of my feet. No more arthritis, headaches, allergies, or pain of any kind! I have since learned by the Word how to fight spiritual battles when the enemy tries to take me down with sickness or disease. Thank God, we were given the power and authority to use His name, and that by His precious blood we are healed!"

—CRC

⌒

"Jesus gave me new lungs at Joan's meeting in Garland, Texas. When Joan prayed for someone with insomnia, I joined in, because I had been having trouble sleeping. Suddenly, I felt my chest collapse, felt a whoosh from above, and my chest started filling with air. I could breathe deeply! I had been having pretty bad shortness of breath, and had not told anyone about it—only Jesus!

"At that same meeting, one of my husband's legs grew out. I saw it grow out! We went to see our family at Thanksgiving and saw many healing miracles, including a cat that was dying. She couldn't keep food down. The vet couldn't figure it out and gave up on her. After we prayed for her, she got up, ate, and kept it down, and now she is completely healed and getting plump!

"Other healings included my sister-in-law and mother-in-law. They were healed from wheat allergies, a knee was healed, and rotator cuffs healed. I was instantly healed of hemorrhoids and a wheat allergy, scoliosis, loss of height, neck injury, and bad knee. About ten days later, an angel came in the night and rotated one of my vertebrae into the correct position. What a huge relief after twenty years of pain! Last summer we watched Frances Hunter on Sid Roth's archives. My frozen shoulders were completely healed. Now, every morning, as soon as I get up, I raise my arms all the way up until my shoulders touch my ears, and praise God!"

—NNC

⌣

"I had two large, hard nodules in my groin area—one the size of a pea, the other shaped like a Brazil nut—right where my lymph nodes are. They had been there for over a year. They were very uncomfortable and sometimes made it difficult to walk and sleep. They bled and produced pus periodically.

"Despite all of my claiming and calling my healing, which had worked for many other ailments in the past—such as headaches, toothaches, head colds, fevers, etc.—these nodules kept getting bigger and bigger. I didn't tell anyone but just continued to trust God that my body would come into line with His Word.

"My two-year-old son also had two large rashes on the backs of his arms; the cause was unknown. The rashes continued to spread and cause him discomfort, as well. I was miffed as to why these ailments were not leaving our bodies. I asked the Lord, 'What am I doing wrong, Father? Your Word is always true and infallible. So, the problem has to be with me. Holy Spirit, please show me what I am doing wrong.'

"A couple weeks ago, I was watching TBN, and Marilyn Hickey came on. She had ministered at my church a few times, and I grew up being told how anointed she was. However, I never really watched her TV show or followed her ministry. On this particular morning, I felt like I needed to watch, and the guest was a lady named Joan Hunter. I had never heard of her. However, as she began to speak, a sweet presence filled my room. As she began to speak about healing and her new book, I knew it was a God moment.

"In the past, I had been somewhat cynical when it came to healing ministries. I am a preacher's kid; and although I was surrounded by some great men and women of God, I have also seen and heard of some weird and sensational things. I have also seen some people, including family members of mine, remain in bondage and sickness for decades. I have seen many people 'fall out' on the floor and come back up just as messed up as they were when they went down, if not worse. I so badly want to see the creative healing and deliverance power of God in people's lives. It grieves me deeply to see people hurt, maimed, crippled, dying, deathly ill, possessed, oppressed, and bound. It makes me so passionately angry, and it hurts my heart to the core.

"My son died in 2006 from an acute and rare form of lymphoma at two years old, and my mother died from breast cancer in 2003. I have two aunts who suffer from extreme mental illness, and two aunts and a cousin who died from various rare forms of cancer. All of these people were believers from a ministry family. That is not okay! It makes me angry to know that Jesus died and took our sicknesses and diseases on Himself, but we, as a whole, are still a broken and defeated people. I long to see people delivered and set free. Where are the people whom God has called to walk unselfishly and successfully in this gift and commission? Who will teach up-and-coming ministers like myself how to walk in this assignment?

"Joan Hunter started to talk about her parents, her spiritual inheritance, the proper way to pray for illnesses and get results, and the book that she had written on the matter. Well, I didn't have the money for the book, but I tuned in and paid attention to every word that came out of her mouth. I was searching for the answer to my plea, 'Holy Spirit, please show me what I'm doing wrong,' and here was my answer! I needed to speak to the root of the issue and curse it, then command my body to be healed, according to the Word of God. It was so simple.

"The enemy told me, 'You need to wait until you can get the book. You might still do it wrong. It can't be that simple. Your family members would have figured that out.'

"I said, 'Shut up, devil! It was that simple for Jesus. So, it's that simple for me. Get away from me!'

"I laid hands on myself, bound the spirit of fear, and commanded the sickness to leave my body. I cursed the infection that was causing the swelling in my groin. I cursed the pus, the bad bacteria, and every other thing that came to my heart to say. (I hadn't gone to the doctor, so I had no 'diagnosis,' but I trusted that the Holy Spirit would teach me all things, according to John 14:26.) I then grabbed my son, laid hands on the rashes, and prayed the same thing. I praised God for the rest of the day, knowing that it was done.

"The next morning, both the nodules in my groin and the rashes on my son's arms were healed—completely gone! Praise God!"

—JBK

⌒

"I went on my vacation to Florida, planning to attend Joan's meetings with my family. They were not excited about going because it was a six-hour drive. I was disappointed because they needed healing. Then it dawned on me that I have been ordained under JHM and I have been trained to pray for the sick. I prayed for all my relatives, and they all got healed. What an exciting vacation!"

⌒

"My daughter came with me to the miracle and healing service at God's Girlz in Conroe. She was healed of hard knots between her neck and shoulders. The next night at work, a young lady twisted her ankle. We prayed; she was healed and worked the rest of the night."

Emotional Healings

"This weekend, I had the privilege and opportunity to attend the three-day impartation and activation conference as a visitor rather than a registered participant. As Joan walked through the healing workbook, it dawned on me at one point that I no longer had bitter feelings toward my husband *at all*. Every feeling of anger and resentment was gone. When I realized that I could not even recall past hurts, I began to cry. For most of the session, I continued to cry, because I didn't realize how bound I had been with unforgiveness. FYI—if ALL the tissue boxes were empty on the left side of the church, it was because of me!

"He and I have been married for almost thirty-seven years. As I sat and tried to remember the hurts, I couldn't! It's as if that part of my memory has been erased.

"The new and renewed love I now have for my husband is incredible. Before, I had such a struggle with speaking words of encouragement or positive words about him. Do you know that he is a genius? He is an incredibly gifted man, and to think that I could not see that for years and years and years (did I mention years?). He is handsome, strong, gifted, and a wonderful husband.

"As I gave it further thought, I had another epiphany…: So many people are bound up in unforgiveness and hurt. So many people are walking around with unresolved issues in their heart. But I now have the tools that I can study so that others can be set free!"

⌣

"As I was listening to your CDs on Erasing the Pain of Your Past, you shared a story where a woman was healed of fibromyalgia; I felt the Lord speak to me inwardly to receive healing. I really didn't even know that was my problem….But I said, 'I receive.'

"I stopped everything I was doing, went into my bedroom, and, for forty-five minutes, felt a cooling sensation go up my spine and across my shoulders. You said on the CD healing angels were ministering, and I knew they were. When I felt a release from the Lord to leave my room, I went on to cook dinner, and went about my evening with the cooling sensation still in my back and shoulders. When I went to sleep, the cooling sensation was still there.

"My son just told me, as we were rejoicing over the healing, 'You are not the same person.' I just had to share with you this glorious report. My husband and I pastor a church here, and for the first time in years, I have boundless energy to do everything God has called me to do. Thank you. Love you and blessings to you and your team."

⌒

"I sent a prayer request for a friend and his family. He has had reconciliation with his in-laws, and God provided a job. This new believer had a great test, but God sustained him. His faith increased and God provided a great job for him. A friend's husband was in prison. He was released without any charge against him. At that time, she found out that she was expecting a baby and had symptoms of complications. After prayer, she gave birth to a healthy, cute baby boy. They all now experience the peace of Jesus."

⌒

"A young lady came for ministry in Ireland. She had lived with severe verbal, mental, and sexual abuse as a teenager. Her father targeted her with frequent physical abuse. Any money she earned was confiscated by her parents. Following ministry, she knew she had to allow God to heal her.

"She often lost sleep because of tormenting nightmares recalling those traumatic events. She blamed herself, just like her family blamed her, for all negative things that happened in her early years. She was tired and weak, and she started getting migraines. She became more and more determined to be free from it all. She was not going to allow the devil to win!

"She came to one of JHM meetings in Ireland. She brought her list of prayer points to the front to be prayed for: (1) torment in my sleep to stop, (2) restoration in my family, (3) to stop feeling worthless, and (4) to not walk in fear anymore.

"Here is the report she gave afterward:

When you prayed for me, you told me everything that had happened to me. I knew something had happened. The pressure had lifted, and I didn't feel weighed down anymore. I wasn't afraid to go to sleep. I haven't had any more nightmares, and the torment has stopped! I haven't had any headaches, and I sleep all throughout the night. I wake up refreshed and ready for each day. My body is stronger than it has been all year! I can truly look back and say, "Wow! God, You have truly amazed me with Your goodness this year! I am FREE!"

"Her relationship with her sister has been restored. She met her father and felt no fear. God was with her, and she was able to tell him she forgave him. She knows she has been totally set free! 'I am safe!' she says. 'I know God is still working behind the scenes to bring restoration to the rest of my family and with my dad.'"

—RTP

Miraculous Provision

"I recently ordered the book *Supernatural Provision* by Joan Hunter and received it in the mail. I am on chapter 8 now. I haven't even finished the book yet and already God is doing wonderful things for me and my husband.

"Earlier this month, we wanted another car. Our 2003 Ford Explorer has been having transmission problems, and we wanted one with better gas mileage. We found a car with the details we wanted nearby. My husband wasn't too pleased with the car's cosmetic problems, so we left it at that. I printed and posted a picture of what we wanted and hung it on our refrigerator. I followed some guidelines Joan mentioned in the book and prayed over it. We made our request known to our Father.

"Suddenly we found another blue 2008 Acura TL with black interior, but this one was even better! The car was in Indiana, and we live in North Carolina. I asked God to make a way for us to go buy it. My husband went to the bank to get a loan, and we got a last-minute flight to Indiana. By ten o'clock the next morning, we were on the road in our new car for the ten-hour drive back home in a snowstorm.

"This car had super-low mileage, blue with black leather interior, just the way we wanted. In a thirty-hour period, God had made a way for us. Our prayers were answered. I thank my Lord Jesus for *Supernatural Provision*."

—BX

〜

"Last Thursday, during a prayer meeting, a woman told us that she had just spent the last of her savings to fill her oil tank, and she had more bills to pay. We were speaking God's provision over her. As others were praying,

I saw a hand with a large pile of coins. It appeared that some of the coins on the top of the stack were disappearing. I told the woman what I saw, and I commanded the demon to stop stealing what God had given and to return what has been stolen. I just learned that when this woman went to her car that same evening, there was a wad of bills worth over $90. She was so excited.

"After sowing seed at the Florida meeting, she received an unexpected check in the mail. After sowing seed and believing all weekend at another meeting, she found out her offer was accepted, and she was able to start purchasing the house next door (her third house). She is turning it into her massage business with a healing room dedicated for prayer, praise, and worship. She got the balance amount of her first home and was able to pay it in full, two years early."

—MVNJ

〜

"Last weekend, I was at the meeting at Ocean Gate Baptist Church in Hawthorne, California, for two of your services. You prayed for me on Friday evening. I'm a worship leader. You prayed for me to get a job, as I've been unemployed for three years, and that I would get new songs.

"You encouraged me to get dressed in my work clothes and be ready for a job on Monday. Although I still don't have a regular job yet, I got a call on that Monday afternoon from a friend, asking me if I could lead worship for a help group at their church that evening. I was paid for it. I believe this is the beginning of God opening doors for me and bringing me a job soon. Also, when I got home from the meetings, the Lord gave me a brand-new worship song. It came in about five to ten minutes—the lyrics, melody, everything."

—JFF

Supernatural Financial Multiplication

"I gave my monthly donation as a partner on the 11th of June of $111.00. Within a few hours, someone handed me $1,111.00. Thank You, Jesus."

—ABH

〜

"I was ordained in October at JHM. I gave in the offering, trusting God for a raise at my job. I went to work the following Monday, and they gave me a $6,000-a-year raise and a bonus. Later I attended another JHM meeting in July and gave what God told me to give. The next day at work, I was given a second raise of over a thousand dollars a month. The two raises equal more than $18,000 a year, not to mention the bonus. He is giving me more finances so I can give more."

—ABI

〜

"I came to a meeting in Nova Scotia and gave all that I had in the offering. It was less than $2. I went home from the service and got out my Bible. I discovered $200 in my Bible!"

〜

"When Joan came to Minnesota, I gave all I had in the offering. (I am a student with no income.) I gave $3, believing for a car from God. We were two hours away from the closest car dealership. Within two days, a car was delivered to me as a gift. Thank You, Jesus! All I needed was money for the insurance for the car. The next day, someone gave me $1,153 as a gift, so I was able to pay for insurance and gas! God is good!"

Supernatural Safety

"The Lord rescued our daughter from a destructive relationship with the wrong guy. I called you this time last year, asking for prayer. The man involved was manipulative and deceptive and didn't love God. Through a miracle that only God could orchestrate, He rescued our daughter and brought her back to Himself. In addition, He gave her a wonderful, godly husband, and they were married last Saturday. Those watching this saw a miracle indeed, too. Thank You, Jesus! Thank you for your prayers, too!"

—CND

If I Can Do It, So Can You

I overheard a discussion among a few employees of Joan Hunter Ministries in which someone began a sentence, "We all know that we do not walk in...." I stepped in and finished the sentence: "...the same anointing and power that I do." I immediately corrected this faulty notion, explaining, "First, you are a believer. God has given all believers the anointing and power to heal the sick. Second, you are under the covering of this ministry. That means that you do walk and pray in the same anointing and power that I walk in, whether at work or at home."

A few days later, the truth of this fact was clearly demonstrated. A lady called the office for prayer. She was extremely determined to talk to me and only me. She was convinced that my prayers alone could help her situation. The phone volunteer finally convinced her to accept prayer from someone other than me. The volunteer later explained, "I started praying for a new back. I could see the spine come into my office through the phone. Suddenly, the lady at the other end of the phone yelled, 'I have a new spine! I have a new spine!'"

Only qualified people monitor the prayer lines at JHM. They have sat under my teachings, have ministered with me, and are mentored on a regular basis. Every employee of JHM completes a series of ordination and impartation classes soon after being hired. We all work in a spirit of total unity, thereby multiplying the anointing and power at work when we minister to others.

The principles we teach at JMH are no different from the steps Jesus set forth in the Bible. This means that you, too, are qualified to minister healing to others! Yes, Jesus is moving through His church—you! God wants to use His children—you! Are you ready? Are you prepared? Are you willing? As we move forward, we will explore the biblical requirements for receiving and ministering the gifts of God, including miraculous healings.

PART II:

CONDITIONS FOR RECEIVING

5

PRESENT YOUR REQUESTS

"Ask, and it will be given to you; seek, and you will find; knock, and it will be opened to you. For everyone who asks receives, and he who seeks finds, and to him who knocks it will be opened."
—Matthew 7:7–8

What are some reasons someone might give you something? Maybe you did someone a favor. Perhaps you entered into a contract agreement—you performed some task in exchange for money or an item you needed. Maybe the elderly neighbor across the street has a large vegetable garden she can no longer take care of, and so you offer to tend the garden in exchange for part of the produce. In doing so, you have earned the right to receive.

Whatever your profession or line of business, the principle is the same. By agreement, work is done in exchange for money, prestige, advancement, or some other commodity. Everyone has a goal. For some, their goal is a stepping-stone to advancement and continued success. For others, the goal may be something as simple as earning enough money to feed their kids this week. The exchange of goods, services, and money is an ongoing cycle on a global scale.

In a family and among close friends, gifts are exchanged during special occasions, such as birthdays and anniversaries. You qualify for a gift, or "prove" your worthiness to receive, just by being "in the family." In general, I don't think you should expect to receive anything pleasant from anyone whom you have treated with anything less than sincere goodwill and godly love; but being family makes a big difference—it covers a multitude of sins.

The same thing is true in the family of God, whose Head is the Almighty Himself. When you pray the salvation prayer, you are adopted, or grafted, into the family of God, who *"decided in advance to adopt us into his own family by bringing us to himself through Jesus Christ. This is what he wanted to do, and it gave him great pleasure"* (Ephesians 1:5 NLT).

God is now your heavenly Father, and Jesus is your Brother. As part of the family, you qualify to receive your inheritance. You can claim the promises God made to Abraham. Your Father owns the cattle on a thousand hills (see Psalm 50:10), and He can certainly supply your needs. Therefore, you can echo Paul's proclamation in Philippians 4:19: *"My God shall supply all* [my] *need according to His riches in glory by Christ Jesus."*

Yours for the Asking

If God gave His only Son for your salvation, you should have no doubt that He will supply what you need today. Jesus' death had a great purpose.

God brought Him through with great victory to provide salvation and redemption for you, and it follows that He desires you to prosper and enjoy good health, so that you may fulfill His call on your life.

However, just as with earthly parents, your heavenly Father may be reluctant to bless you if your attitude is not right. When you live in such a way as to attract His favor, and you learn how to receive from Him, your life will make a complete turnaround.

We will discuss the conditions for receiving and maintaining miracles from God, as well as habits and heart attitudes to avoid because they block His blessings. First, we are going to discuss step one in receiving, and that's asking. It is only logical that we should not expect to receive what we have not asked for!

Answer the Call to Pray

If miracles aren't happening at your church or in your immediate circle, someone is not answering the call to pray and expect great things from God. God answers prayer; and if there are no prayers going up, God is not required to send any blessings down. Many may be receiving blessings from Him, but not talking about it at all. God needs to get the glory from His children. Encourage one another to share what God is doing. Build each other up to do more.

God needs to get the glory from His children. Encourage one another to share what God is doing. Build each other up to do more.

Some don't pray for the sick because their "faith" rests in doctors; only when the doctors have given up on someone do they turn to God and search for a church where the people lay hands on the sick and see them recover. Now, I am not against consulting a doctor when I feel it is necessary, because God sometimes heals His children through the treatment of professional physicians. But God doesn't know failure. He gives you directions to follow. Your responsibility is to obey and pray. God has to fulfill His promises and complete the healing miracle!

Asking Effectively

Ask, and it will be given to you; seek, and you will find; knock, and it will be opened to you. For everyone who asks receives, and he who seeks finds, and to him who knocks it will be opened. Or what man is there among you who, if his son asks for bread, will give him a stone? Or if he asks for a fish, will he give him a serpent? If you then, being evil, know how to give good gifts to your children, how much more will your Father who is in heaven give good things to those who ask Him! Therefore, whatever you want men to do to you, do also to them, for this is the Law and the Prophets. (Matthew 7:7–12)

Just like Jesus said, "*Ask,…seek,…knock, and it will be opened to you.*" Earthly parents do everything in their power to help their children succeed. Don't you think God is the same? By His help, man has made great strides in developing into what we are today. He is ready to help, if you will only ask.

Many people give the excuse that they don't know how to ask. As God says in Hosea 4:6, "*My people are destroyed for lack of knowledge.*" In today's technological society, lack of education is a poor excuse. People from around the world listen and watch via the Internet to teachings and conferences available in numerous languages. Knowledge is available 24/7. Many ministry teachings are available by video or on the Internet.

Many other great and anointed ministries are available also. Ask God who you need to listen to and learn from. Tune in and learn.

As a child of the King, you are walking in His authority. You have been given the privilege of using Jesus' name, which entitles you to His power. In this chapter, I will cover some of the basics of proper petitions that receive answers—whether prayers for yourself or intercession on behalf of others.

Converse with God

Some people mistakenly believe that the louder the prayer, the more effective it will be. Some assume weeping and wailing in intercession is the correct approach to reach God's ears and bring down His blessings. It isn't.

A child of God doesn't have to plead or beg. How outrageous to think that God requires this type of behavior before releasing His love!

Praying may be done quite effectively in your prayer closet when you are alone in your secret place. And you need not yell or scream. Praying is a two-way conversation. When you are making so much noise, you will never hear from God, because He speaks with a *"still small voice"* (1 Kings 19:12).

Be Specific

Vague, generic prayers don't always produce the desired results because they aren't measurable. If you pray for "blessings," you can't tell if your prayer was answered; whereas if you pray for a healing that manifests, you know God answered your prayer. At my ministry, through the years, we have learned that successful prayers need to be as specific as possible. The more specific your prayers are, the better the results tend to be! Of course, if complete details are not available, generic prayer is better than no prayer at all.

This is another reason I support visiting the doctor—a doctor's diagnosis can help make your prayers more effective because it lets you know specifically what you ought to pray for.

This is another reason I support visiting the doctor—a doctor's diagnosis can help make your prayers more effective because it lets you know specifically what you ought to pray for. Instead of a generic prayer, such as, "Father, heal this person of leg pain," you can zero in on the cause and say, "I curse the spirit of arthritis. It has to go, in Jesus' name. I speak new cartilage into the joint, and pain is gone, in Jesus' name!" Whatever the doctors diagnose, turn it into a list of prayer concerns.

Never Doubt God's Will

In some religious circles, the belief is that sickness is God's way of purifying the soul from evil and providing the person with spiritual object lessons in humility and love. They truly believe that God has caused the illness or problems they are facing. In this case, praying against what God wants for

Be confident in God's Word, and you will see the sick recover. You will see His miracles manifest.

the person is positioning you against God's will—somewhere you don't want to be. It doesn't even make sense. If someone is in abject poverty and ill, they aren't there because of God. He walks in love.

Some people minister and pray with such doubt, it is obvious they are not convinced of God's ability or desire to heal. They say, "If it be Your will," and it sounds so humble. But this phrase reveals a lack of faith. If you lack confidence in God's ability to answer your prayers, you need to go back to the Bible and study what it has to say about His plan for your life. If you want to recover from an illness or be financially blessed, you must kick doubt right out the door. God desires that His children walk in health and prosperity. The Bible is full of assurances that He wants all His children to be successful and prosperous in every area of their lives.

No one who prays using the phrase "if it be Your will" should expect success when ministering to the sick. You must be totally convinced that God wants His children well and healthy. Be confident in God's Word, and you will see the sick recover. You will see His miracles manifest.

A friend of mine from England has been in the healing ministry for more than fifteen years. Early on in his ministry, about three of every hundred people he prayed for were healed. After he attended a healing school my ministry held at his church, he started averaging sixty out of every hundred people getting healed. That's not the 100 percent I strive for; however, even when I reach 100 percent, I still won't be satisfied. I want to see God do even more. I want Him to exceed my expectations. I'm not satisfied yet, and I am never going to quit.

When a blind person is healed, I don't say, "That's all I wanted to do. I'm going to sit down because I'm done." No, I keep on ministering, praying for healing in other areas, as well. After a great service, I don't simply say, "That's it" and sit down. I keep going. I have a greater determination today than ever before to do what God has called me to do.

The same anointing is yours, if you are a child of God; and whatever God ordains or plans for your life, He will supply the finances, the education, and the means for you to fulfill. Simply allow His anointing to work through you.

Consider Fasting

Fasting, as God directs, allows you to spend more time with Him and to enjoy a deeper intimacy, which is important in the realm of prayer. As you give up or avoid some creature comforts, you can keep your focus on Him and His will.

Fasting usually brings up thoughts of not eating for days; however, other things can be "fasted" from, also. What about staying away from the distraction of television or thousands of Internet sites that don't proclaim the name of Jesus? Many worldly things threaten to distract you from your walk and concentration on the things of God, and media fasts are one way to sever the grip that the world has on you.

Fasting from food gives you an opportunity to feed on the Word. If you listen to the world continuously, your faith will starve to death; but if you listen to the Word continuously, your faith will thrive. Surround yourself with men and women of God who believe in healing and who will feed your spirit with God's precious Word. Listening to worship music and making time to sing praises to God will also feed your spirit, because worship opens a direct line to the heart of God.

Pray Together with Other Believers

James 5:16 instructs us, *"Pray for one another, that you may be healed. The effective, fervent prayer of a righteous [person] avails much."* If you're having a very hard time with a broken heart, find somebody who is going through the same situation and pray for that person. Then, ask that person to pray for you. If you are having financial problems, find somebody who is having financial problems, and pray for each other, that each of you will be set free financially.

There is also power in agreement. Jesus said, *"If two of you agree on earth concerning anything that they ask, it will be done for them by My Father in heaven. For where two or three are gathered together in My name, I am there in the midst of them"* (Matthew 18:19–20).

Be Persistent

Praying for one another and believing for incredible outcomes is completely scriptural, even if the results do not manifest immediately. I remember my mother, Frances Hunter, telling me that the first five people she prayed for died. So, what did she do? She just kept praying for the sick. She obeyed God. It was God's responsibility to heal them, not hers.

What if my parents had given up on the ministry? How many hundreds of thousands of people around the world would not be healed today? If they had quit so easily, how many hundreds of thousands of people would not have the baptism of the Holy Spirit?

That could be true for you, as well. It is so easy to quit, but it is fun being in the middle of what God has called you to do. Stay in the flow of the Holy Spirit. Some people have gotten off track or have been blocked by problems, whether financial, spiritual, or emotional. If necessary, pray for a breakthrough in your life.

Many people reading this have been called into the ministry. You were involved in ministry in the past, but you are no longer doing that now. Some of you have been involved in ministry and have just shut down because of opposition. Is that you? You can receive a paycheck from a secular company and still be involved in Christian ministry.

You may have had to deal with a lot of opposition, pain, and disappointment. I've been through hell, but it's a whole lot better being on the other side. Don't give up. Simply release your cares to the Lord through prayer. "Be anxious for nothing, but in everything by prayer and supplication, with thanksgiving, let your requests be made known to God" (Philippians 4:6).

Pray in the Name of Jesus

If you ask anything in My name, I will do it.　　　　　(John 14:14)

You did not choose Me, but I chose you and appointed you that you should go and bear fruit, and that your fruit should remain, that whatever you ask the Father in My name He may give you.　　(John 15:16)

Most assuredly, I say to you, whatever you ask the Father in My name He will give you. Until now you have asked nothing in My name. Ask, and you will receive, that your joy may be full.　　(John 16:23–24)

Jesus was very clear that you are to use His name in presenting your requests to your heavenly Father. The first disciple to use the name of Jesus as a tool for healing was Peter. He and John were headed to the temple for prayer when they came upon a lame beggar. When the man asked them for alms, Peter replied, *"Silver and gold I do not have, but what I do have I give you:* **In the name of Jesus Christ** *of Nazareth rise up and walk"* (Acts 3:6).

Jesus told His disciples that they could use His name to do whatever miracles needed to be done, but up until this point, it was strictly "head knowledge." Jesus had said, "I give you the right to use My name. I give you power of attorney to use My name. Use it for whatever circumstances you need to use it, as often as you like, as many times as you like."

What a gift for the faithful followers of Jesus! Someone with a power of attorney can act in place of the person—in this case, Jesus. Jesus had such faith that His disciples would follow and act in His behalf. No restrictions, no rules; He trusted them to do exactly the same as He would do if He were present. What a significant recognition of Jesus' faith in man.

Years ago, my parents held large meetings at which it was literally impossible to lay hands on every sick person. My mother would wave her hand over the audience and say, "Be healed, in Jesus' name!" It seemed most of the audience would get hit with Holy Spirit power and fall back into their chairs. They would stand up sometime later, completely healed.

Jesus' name is powerful. It is the name above every name.

Therefore God also has highly exalted Him and given Him the name which is above every name, that at the name of Jesus every knee should bow, of those in heaven, and of those on earth, and of those under the earth, and that every tongue should confess that Jesus Christ is Lord, to the glory of God the Father. (Philippians 2:9–12)

Jesus has given you His name, also. You have His power of attorney. What is stopping you from using it and claiming God's best?

Just Pray!

The only thing that can keep you from seeing others healed is not praying for them. Even if you do not know what to say, the Holy Spirit will fill in
the blanks.

*Likewise the Spirit also helps in our weaknesses. For we do not know what
we should pray for as we ought, but the Spirit Himself makes intercession
for us with groanings which cannot be uttered. Now He who searches the
hearts knows what the mind of the Spirit is, because He makes intercession for the saints according to the will of God.* (Romans 8:26–27)

*When you are arrested, don't worry about how to respond or what to
say. God will give you the right words at the right time.*
(Matthew 10:19 NLT)

*For I will give you the right words and such wisdom that none of your
opponents will be able to reply or refute you!* (Luke 21:15 NLT)

Before moving on, please agree with me in the following prayer:

Father, right now, in the name of Jesus, I loose those reading this
book, in Jesus' name, and I release them into the ministry to which
You have called them. Father, I thank You that You are the God of
mercy and grace, in Jesus' name. Father, I speak a special anointing
on them, in Jesus' name. Father, I thank You for giving them peace
such as they have never experienced. I speak peace and strength into
their heart and wholeness where men have tried to destroy them. I
ask these things in Jesus' name.

Father, I thank You for providing clear guidance as to what these
dear children of Yours are to do. Father, in the name of Jesus, I loose
their finances. I thank You for healing their body and restoring all
that the enemy has stolen.

Father, in the name of Jesus, I thank You for equipping us to with-
stand against the opposition of the enemy. We stand in agreement

for those that are participants in this ministry. Father, I thank You for those who come alongside Your ministers. I stir up the gift of determination. I ask that You would plant an extra seed of faith into every single person who reads this book, in Jesus' name. I come against all opposition to Your call on their lives. Any hindrances to receiving are broken off and will melt away under the power of the Holy Spirit.

Father, I thank You that they are more determined to do what You have called them to do and that You are going to give them greater grace to persevere than they have ever had before. Thank You for giving them greater wisdom and knowledge in their businesses, in their jobs, and in their ministries, in Jesus' name. I speak prosperity over them, not only financially, but in every area of their lives. Father, bless their socks off. Speak to them with greater revelation than they have ever known before. Amen and amen.

Your healed heart is going to open up doors for powerful ministry to the body of Christ. Thousands of people need to be set free. Filled with His power, how can you lose? Open those doors! Heal the sick! Set the captives free! The Holy Spirit will guide you every step of the way.

6

POSITION YOURSELF
TO RECEIVE

"I will instruct you and teach you in the way you should go;
I will counsel you and watch over you."
—Psalm 32:8 (NIV)

I f your car needs gas, do you stand in your house and fuss and fume?
No, you head to the nearest gas station and refuel. Likewise, if your

family is hungry but the pantry is empty, what do you do? You go to the grocery store—or maybe you opt for dinner out at a restaurant, instead. You can't get gas from a restaurant or a sit-down dinner at a gas station. You have to know where to go to acquire what you want.

In the same way, if there is something you need from your heavenly Father—be it monetary provision, physical healing, or a restored relationship—you need to position yourself in the right place to receive it. As you will see, the positioning process has as much to do with the condition of your heart as it does the location of your body.

Just as you have to be in the right place to refuel your car or purchase groceries, you must be in the right place to receive God's blessings. As the saying goes, "Get under the spout where His blessings come out."

Get in the Right Place, Physically

A good example of someone positioning himself to receive from the Lord is the prophet Elijah, who had to move to the place where God could provide for his sustenance. In 1 Kings 17, God speaks to Elijah, saying, "*Get away from here and turn eastward, and hide by the Brook Cherith, which flows into the Jordan. And it will be that you shall drink from the brook, and I have commanded the ravens to feed you there*" (1 Kings 17:3–4). Elijah followed those instructions and found life-giving sustenance in water from the brook and meat delivered by ravens. (See 1 Kings 17:6.)

After a while, the brook ran dry, and God spoke to him again, with these directions: "*Arise, go to Zarephath, which belongs to Sidon, and dwell there. See, I have commanded a widow there to provide for you*" (1 Kings 17:9). Again, Elijah obeyed; sure enough, he came upon a widow who was not well off but whose fortunes soon improved thanks to a miracle.

[The widow] *said, "As the LORD your God lives, I do not have bread, only a handful of flour in a bin, and a little oil in a jar; and see, I am gathering a couple of sticks that I may go in and prepare it for myself and my son, that we may eat it, and die." And Elijah said to her, "Do not fear; go and do as you have said, but make me a small cake from it first, and bring it to me; and afterward make some for yourself and your son. For thus says the LORD God of Israel: 'The bin of flour shall not be used up, nor shall the jar of oil run dry, until the day the LORD sends rain on the earth.'" So she went away and did according to the word of Elijah; and she and he and her household ate for many days. The bin of flour was not used up, nor did the jar of oil run dry, according to the word of the LORD which He spoke by Elijah.* (1 Kings 17:12–16)

God wants to bless you with miracles, but you may need to go elsewhere to receive them. Whether it arrives in your own backyard or halfway across the globe, God's provision for you is found in the center of His perfect will.

He provides for what He ordains, and He places you in a position to receive it, if you will only obey Him, as did Elijah and the widow in 1 Kings 17. Elijah followed God's instructions, and the widow fulfilled His orders as given through Elijah. She gave what little she had, and God blessed her with more than enough by multiplying her gift back to her and prolonging the life of herself and her son. What a wonderful demonstration of God's multiplication of return!

Get in the Right Place, Spiritually

In addition to physically being in the correct position, you must be in the correct place, spiritually. This "place" is found when you humble yourself and tune your heart to hear from God.

Now it shall come to pass, if you diligently obey the voice of the LORD your God, to observe carefully all His commandments which I command you today, that the LORD your God will set you high above all nations of the earth. And all these blessings shall come upon you and overtake you, because you obey the voice of the LORD your God. (Deuteronomy 28:1–2)

Have you studied His Word in regard to your personal situation? Have you opened your heart to hear what He has to say about your healing, your financial challenges, or your family situation? If not, "position" yourself on your knees for a while and call out to God. "Position" yourself in your secret place and listen. "Position" yourself to meet God—physically, emotionally, and spiritually.

> But you, when you pray, go into your room, and when you have shut your
> door, pray to your Father who is in the secret place; and your Father who
> sees in secret will reward you openly. (Matthew 6:6)

> He who dwells in the secret place of the Most High shall abide under the
> shadow of the Almighty. (Psalm 91:1)

Sometimes, being in the right place, spiritually, involves adjusting the noise level. Can you hear God and see His handiwork in the midst of your life, however crazy, noisy, and busy it may be? Sometimes you may; however, usually you will have to separate yourself and be alone with Him. Even though He is a great big God, His voice doesn't boom across the sky. He speaks in whispers of gentleness and kindness. He waits for you to come to Him. He wants to be invited. He is a Gentleman who won't interfere with your business. You have to choose to listen.

> *Even though He is a*
> *great big God,*
> *His voice doesn't boom*
> *across the sky. He*
> *speaks in whispers of*
> *gentleness and kindness.*
> *He waits for you to*
> *come to Him.*

Find a quiet place to meet with Him. Welcome the Holy Spirit into your life and your home. Invite Him to envelop your existence. He loves to talk and commune with you. He is your Helper, your Guide, and your Best Friend forever. He will tell you where to be and what to say. Learn to receive in your secret place in God's presence. You are worthy because He makes you worthy. Read His Word, surround yourself with beautiful worship music, and sing praises to the One who alone is worthy.

Positioned in Obedience

Are you in the correct place? Are you in the center of God's will or just dabbling at the edges? What was the last thing He told you to do? If you didn't obey at that time, you may need to go back and finish that task before He gives you another word. Obedience is important.

> *A certain woman of the wives of the sons of the prophets cried out to Elisha, saying, "Your servant my husband is dead, and you know that your servant feared the* LORD. *And the creditor is coming to take my two sons to be his slaves." So Elisha said to her, "What shall I do for you? Tell me, what do you have in the house?" And she said, "Your maidservant has nothing in the house but a jar of oil." Then he said, "Go, borrow vessels from everywhere, from all your neighbors; empty vessels; do not gather just a few. And when you have come in, you shall shut the door behind you and your sons; then pour it into all those vessels, and set aside the full ones." So she went from him and shut the door behind her and her sons, who brought the vessels to her; and she poured it out. Now it came to pass, when the vessels were full, that she said to her son, "Bring me another vessel." And he said to her, "There is not another vessel." So the oil ceased. Then she came and told the man of God. And he said, "Go, sell the oil and pay your debt; and you and your sons live on the rest.*
>
> (2 Kings 4:1–7)

Elisha instructed the widow to sell as much oil as needed to pay off her debt, and to use the remainder for money to live on. God multiplied what she had so she could pay off her debt and have enough to last her and her son for the rest of their days. Had she ignored Elisha and neglected to obey his instructions, the oil would not have multiplied. If she had borrowed even more containers, she could have been blessed even more.

She had cried out for help, and God supplied her need in a supernatural way. The widow did not disqualify herself or refuse to be obedient because of pride or social status. She obeyed, and she received exactly what she had been praying and believing God for.

Regardless of what it looks like in the natural, obedience to God is always the proper position for receiving His best. When you are in the

Regardless of what it looks like in the natural, obedience to God is always the proper position for receiving His best.

center of His will, you are perfectly positioned for the overflow of His abundant blessings.

When you receive divine direction from God in the form of a word from Him, you should say, "At Your word, I will do whatever You tell me to do." When you instantly obey God without question, it pleases Him. Don't attempt to find another way to do something. Don't come up with a list of excuses not to follow His lead. God knows what is best.

When He sends a blessing, suddenly you find all you need. God always provides for you. He has more than just enough waiting for His children. Believe that He will give you everything you need. Act on His prophetic word, obey His written Word, and then open your heart and arms to receive!

Positioned at the Feet of Jesus

And when Jesus was in Bethany at the house of Simon the leper, a woman came to Him having an alabaster flask of very costly fragrant oil, and she poured it on His head as He sat at the table. But when His disciples saw it, they were indignant, saying, "Why this waste? For this fragrant oil might have been sold for much and given to the poor." But when Jesus was aware of it, He said to them, "Why do you trouble the woman? For she has done a good work for Me. For you have the poor with you always, but Me you do not have always. For in pouring this fragrant oil on My body, she did it for My burial. Assuredly, I say to you, wherever this gospel is preached in the whole world, what this woman has done will also be told as a memorial to her."
(Matthew 26:6–13; see also Mark 14:3–9; Luke 7:37–50)

Jesus was known by many people and loved by most. However, the Pharisees were looking for a way to trap Him or comment on where and with whom He spent His time. When Jesus was at Bethany, a woman with a bad reputation came to pour oil on His head. As she worshipped Him, her tears of sorrow washed His feet, and she used her hair to dry them. (See Matthew 26:7; Mark 14:3; Luke 7:37.)

The oil contained within the alabaster box that was broken was used on Jesus in preparation for His burial. No one knew what that week would hold.

The short-sighted disciples could only criticize her for "wasting" it on Jesus instead of selling it and giving the money to the poor. They were caught up in what other things that gift could be used for, rather than seeing the beautiful act of worship playing out in front of them.

Jesus corrected them, saying, *"You will always have the poor among you, but you will not always have me"* (John 12:8 NIV). He knew that His time on earth was about to end; every moment was precious. Jesus received the oil and her tears. He recognized her act of worship. She needed to be forgiven, and with her worship also came forgiveness.

Let's consider yet another woman who discovered blessings at the feet of Jesus.

> *Now it happened as they went that He entered a certain village; and a certain woman named Martha welcomed Him into her house. And she had a sister called Mary, who also sat at Jesus' feet and heard His word. But Martha was distracted with much serving, and she approached Him and said, "Lord, do You not care that my sister has left me to serve alone? Therefore tell her to help me." And Jesus answered and said to her, "Martha, Martha, you are worried and troubled about many things. But one thing is needed, and Mary has chosen that good part, which will not be taken away from her."* (Luke 10:38–42)

Martha believed she was in the right place—the kitchen. After all, Jesus was her Houseguest, and she was understandably concerned with making adequate preparations for Him! But she prioritized serving over sitting, until Jesus set her straight. Serving is wonderful; ministry is great; but nothing compares to sitting at the feet of Jesus. This act of worship blesses Him, and it blesses you. When you don't know where to go, the feet of Jesus is always the best place to be.

Once You Are In Position...

Have you asked Jesus into your heart? Are you following His guidelines? Are you in the middle of His plan for your life? Will you allow Him to work through you? If so, then you have access to an account that's overflowing with the outpouring of His blessings—financial, physical, and otherwise. Yet there are some keys to keep in mind as you endeavor to withdraw from this account.

Set Goals with Divine Guidance

Daily, people are offered the opportunity to go to work or to pursue a chosen career path. Choices made along that path determine the direction of every life. Plans to marry, buy a house, have kids, and retire by a certain age are all steps along the ladder of a lifetime. The variety of plans is as diverse as the people you encounter on a daily basis.

You can be certain of one thing: God will never withhold any good thing from you. He is a loving and merciful Father.

If your desire is to be in full-time ministry, have you written a business plan and prayed about how and where you will use His blessings? Are you preparing for what He wants you to do? Maybe you need to study a new language before He can send you to minister in another country. Ask Him what you need to do. But do something toward your goal every day. Plan, plan, plan. Write down your plans. Rework them occasionally as you move forward. Be open to His suggestions (not man's criticism).

> And then God answered: "Write this. Write what you see. Write it out in big block letters so that it can be read on the run. This vision-message is a witness pointing to what's coming. It aches for the coming—it can hardly wait! And it doesn't lie. If it seems slow in coming, wait. It's on its way. It will come right on time." (Habakkuk 2:2–3 MSG)

You must be mobile, agile, and hostile! Christians should be ready to move (mobile) whenever God says "Go," healthy enough (agile) to go where God sends them, and prepared (hostile) to recognize and fight the battles the enemy will undoubtedly use in his attempts to interfere with God's plans for your life.

Discern from Whom to Receive

While God is your ultimate Provider, Source, and Sustainer, He often uses other people as conduits to direct His blessings to you. However, you should not assume that everyone who is ready to give you something has your best interests at heart. Even if you are in a position to receive something free of charge—a gift—you should evaluate the source in the same way you would in planning to make a purchase. You are careful with how you spend your hard-earned money, and you must be equally careful when it comes to accepting gifts from others. Discernment is crucial, especially when deciding from which church, ministry, or leader you should receive spiritual guidance.

Discernment is crucial, especially when deciding from which church, ministry, or leader you should receive spiritual guidance.

When I find myself in need of a product or service, my first thought is, *Where should I go to get this? Who will provide the best quality for the best price at the exact time I need it?* For example, when I need a new computer, I seek out an expert in the electronics field. When I need a wardrobe update, I head to my favorite clothing store and consult the associates there. And when I need counsel for spiritual matters, I contact someone I trust who will speak into my life from the heart of God—someone with a proven track record of hearing from God. If someone comes to me with a "word" from God, I want to know who he is. Many of the "words" that have been spoken over me were not from God, and I had to cut them off instead of receive them.

Most people in the process of choosing a surgeon or other health care specialist will thoroughly check out the prospective doctor, demanding to know his credentials and asking for access to written testimonies of former patients. Here is a question to consider: Do you conduct the same research and uphold the same standards when searching for a church home or a ministry to support as you would when seeking a new health care provider? The decisions you make in this regard are just as important, if not more so, for they have the potential to impact your eternal destiny.

If you find yourself seeking a new church home, a spiritual mentor, or a ministry to support, consider asking the following questions: "What is the reputation of this minister/ministry?" "What evidence or fruit has been borne as a result of God working through this minister/ministry?" "Are the doctrinal views and core beliefs of this minister/ministry in alignment with Scripture?"

Depending on the nature of your relationship with this minister or ministry, you may find yourself in a position to give financial gifts, and you want to make sure you are planting seed in good ground likely to yield a bountiful harvest for the kingdom of God.

Ask Him where to go to learn about His Word and how to live by His principles. You may think, *I can just go to the church down the street.* But it is never that simple. Please check out whatever church you plan to attend. Make sure they are teaching the Word of God and not the traditions of man. Unfortunately, some churches in this generation are tickling the ears of the congregation with watered-down, often misinterpreted truths from the hearts of men instead of the heart of God.

With the Internet and church Web sites, anyone can read the vision statement of a church, review the experience and training of the church leadership, and be familiar with the church's activities before attending a service. Do they have a mission statement? Do they give to missions? Do they have ministry for small children as well as the senior population of the community? Who are the apostolic elders who oversee the workings of the church? These elders are usually not members of the church but are responsible for the spiritual oversight of the church functions and leaders. National offices are the heads of the denominational churches and hold to similar beliefs across their church base. Interdenominational or nondenominational churches will choose spiritual leaders with like beliefs to be their overseers.

For instance, church leaders who went to Rhema Bible Training College will function and follow the pattern of Kenneth Hagin and his teachings. His graduate students have started churches around the world as well as gone into individual ministry. Oral Roberts University has thousands of graduates around the world, myself included, who are spreading the Word of God from the teaching we received during our studies at ORU.

Many churches frown on attending or listening to other Christian leaders. Pray for them. No church has all the answers on every subject. The great variety of ministries is scriptural. God says He will give us gifts. One may have insights into the end times, while another's gift may be prophesying.

According to the fivefold ministry gifts, as outlined in the Scriptures (see Ephesians 4:11–12), some will be teachers, pastors, preachers, prophets, and apostles, to equip the saints for the work of the ministry and to edify the body of Christ. There are those with gifts of administration, service, and music. (See 1 Corinthians 12:28–30.) There are many areas of gifts from God. My parents' ministry primarily involved healing and the baptism in the Holy Spirit. Yes, I walk in those same gifts; however, God has added to those gifts, expanding the gift of healing into all areas of life, as well as making me an apostle. I also prophesy.

Find a source where you can listen and learn the Word. There are an abundance of meetings, conventions, TV programs, Internet Web sites as well as churches available to you. Don't hesitate to inquire of the pastor and the other leaders of a church. Make sure they believe the Bible is the divine Word of God, inspired by the Holy Spirit. Check out their beliefs. Once you are satisfied with their qualifications, relax and let God minister to you through them.

Once you have identified teachers who speak to you in a meaningful way, listen to them regularly. You can't visit church once and know everything. Just like you can't eat once and live forever; you must have regular meals of spiritual food to survive and grow in God.

Discern When to Receive

Again, when you believe God to meet a need, you have to understand that in many cases, He must work through other people to supply the finances in answer to your prayers. It will take God moving on the hearts of people around you to get you from simply "believing" to actually "receiving."

The best reason to receive is when that gift is given to you freely and without conditions.

How do you know when you should receive gifts of any kind from people around you? The best reason to receive is when that gift is given to you freely and without conditions. God freely gives you the spiritual gifts of salvation and forgiveness; there is nothing you can do to earn them. Jesus freely died on the cross for your salvation and took the punishment for your sins. His death paid the price of provision for forgiveness. It is truly a debt you can never repay.

We see this evidenced in Luke 21:1–4:

> [Jesus] *looked up and saw the rich putting their gifts into the treasury, and He saw also a certain poor widow putting in two mites. So He said, "Truly I say to you that this poor widow has put in more than all; for all these out of their abundance have put in offerings for God, but she out of her poverty put in all the livelihood that she had."*

Jesus honored the widow for giving all that she had to God. Not considering her feelings or her age, people pushed by her as they continued to the altar to give their offering. She gently and quietly gave two copper coins and turned to walk away. She knew the importance of giving and, even more, understood what a sacrificial gift her two mites represented. Trusting God to supply her every need, she gave all that she had to honor Him.

Be willing to be blessed by those around you. Be thankful when people around you have seen your need and offer their help. Do not let pride keep you from accepting a gift.

When you have been praying for God to answer a specific need, and the answer is being given, always thank God for supplying your needs. Never become complacent in your praise and adoration of God. You must always remember He is the Lover of your soul, your Abba Father, your Provider. You are His child, and every good and perfect thing comes from Him. (See James 1:17.)

7

DEVELOP GODLY DETERMINATION

"And suddenly, a woman who had a flow of blood for twelve years came
from behind and touched the hem of His garment.
For she said to herself, 'If only I may touch His garment,
I shall be made well.' But Jesus turned around, and when He saw her
He said, 'Be of good cheer, daughter; your faith has made you well.'
And the woman was made well from that hour."
—Matthew 9:20–22

Themes account of the woman with the issue of blood, also recorded in the Gospels of Mark and Luke, is the story of a woman after my own heart. She exhibited godly determination to get well, and Jesus rewarded her faith by healing her.

This woman with an issue of blood had suffered with abnormal bleeding for years and spent all her money on doctors, who had finally given up on her. She was considered an outcast and could not mingle with other people. According to the Jewish law, not even her husband could touch her. She couldn't care for or hug her children. She lived isolated, alone, and broke.

Imagine you were this woman, lying in a bed year after year, slowly but continually bleeding for twelve years. Even four or five days with a bleeding problem will leave you quite weak and anemic. After twelve years with this problem, it was a miracle she was still alive. She had done everything possible in the natural to get well, including spending all her money on doctors and various medications. It appears that the doctors gave up on her when her money ran out.

One day, though she was very tired and still sick, she got up, bounced out of bed, and ran into the other room. She turned on her laptop and checked online to see where Jesus was speaking that day. She got dressed up in her finest outfit, had her hair done just right, put on a little perfume, and jumped into her new Lexus to go to the meeting. I might add that she also had a reputation as a really neat lady in the greater Jerusalem area. When she got to the meeting, she sat in the front row—because, naturally, she had a reserved seat, and the ushers knew her by name.

Is that what you think happened? No, that's not what occurred at all.

What actually happened? A woman who had suffered for twelve years with a bleeding condition was so weak, she couldn't even get out of bed some days. Her skin was pale, her muscles had shriveled, and her bones were very prominent. She looked both listless and lifeless. Then, she heard about a Man who could heal with a touch of His hand, and a seed of faith was planted in her heart. How did she find out that Jesus was in the area? She probably heard about Him through the most powerful thing in the world: the tongue. Somebody had told her. Friends and relatives may have talked about Him and the mighty miracles that accompanied Him. There is power in the tongue. She listened and believed. She grabbed hold of those words she had heard. Word of mouth was the mode of communication in those days. There were no newspapers, phones, TV, radio, or Internet. People talked and shared and visited one another frequently. Events such as Jesus healing the sick must have spread widely and quickly.

I imagine that another woman visited her and said, "I heard that Jesus is coming by today." Hearing this, the woman got up but could barely walk. She may have crawled on her knees and pushed herself up with her arms until finally she could stand up. She probably stumbled a little bit, here and there, as she tried to balance. Eventually she got dressed in whatever ragged clothes she still possessed and made her way to the door. She went out into the city, despite the people yelling "Unclean!" at her; but there was no map to the place where Jesus was ministering. She had to be determined beyond all comprehension to keep taking one more step after the other to reach her destination. She didn't have taxi fare. She didn't even have money for water or food. I imagine this woman was walking in a slow, unsteady manner as she tried to find Jesus.

Fortunately, she had awakened that morning with a greater determination than she had ever possessed before that day. That seed of faith was growing as she kept repeating, "If I can just but touch His clothes, I will be healed. If I just touch the hem of His garment, I will be made whole."

She might have crawled to His side. She may have had to push and shove through the crowd. However she did it, she made it to the feet of Jesus. Hoping no one would see her or stop her, she reached out to touch the hem of the Master's garment.

Immediately, her bleeding stopped. She knew that she was healed. Jesus felt power had left Him, and He turned around to ask the crowd, "Who touched My clothes?" His confused disciples said to Him, "There are so many people touching You. What do You mean?" Jesus scanned the surrounding faces to find the person who had literally drawn power from Him.

The woman knew what had happened and fell at Jesus' feet as she told Him her story. I can just imagine the loving smile and gentle look Jesus gave her as He reached out to help her to her feet and replied, "Daughter, your faith has made you well. Go in peace and be healed of your affliction."

Determined Faith

Every miracle that Jesus did, including the healing of the woman with the flow of blood, reminds me that absolutely nothing is impossible with God, if you will only believe. This demonstrates not that miracles *can* happen but that they *will* happen. This is one of the most important things to remember in receiving or maintaining a miracle in any area of life.

> *Jesus answered and said to them, "Have faith in God. For assuredly, I say to you, whoever says to this mountain, 'Be removed and be cast into the sea,' and does not doubt in his heart, but believes that those things he says will be done, he will have whatever he says. Therefore I say to you, whatever things you ask when you pray, believe that you receive them, and you will have them."* (Mark 11:22–24)

Don't focus on your problems. Instead, rejoice in all your victories. There will always be problems. Call them what they are—challenges. Challenges are actually opportunities to overcome and shine for Jesus with victory.

Pray God's will. Thank Him for what He is doing in your life. Thank Him for your total healing. Thank Him for your prosperity, even if it hasn't manifested yet. Keep your eyes on God and your future, not on the present circumstances around you. Then, like the woman with the issue of blood, you will be able to stand with faith in the face of...

Physical Limitations

I wonder how many times the woman with the issue of blood collapsed on her way to Jesus. How many times did she want to give up along the way? This frail, tiny woman was so sick, she could barely get out of bed; but she pushed her way through a mass of humanity to touch the edge of Jesus' garment. She didn't allow her infirmity to stop her. She was determined to get through the numerous feet and legs and nameless faces separating her from her miracle. She was done staying in solitary isolation, away from people. She wanted to live again. She chose the path God had waiting for her.

As sick and weak as she was, this woman was determined to find Jesus and receive her healing. How many times did she stumble and fall? How much pain did she inflict on her knees as she searched for Him? I've walked the streets of Jerusalem, and I know that the older parts of the city are not paved, even today. The streets and sidewalks were all uneven, and I am sure it must have been worse two thousand years ago. There was nothing leisurely or pleasant about her journey over the jagged rocks and stones on that road, not to mention the animal droppings that were surely scattered along the way. Yet she pushed through and received complete healing because of her faith and perseverance.

Poor Excuses

Imagine if the woman with the flow of blood had neglected to pursue her healing because she simply "didn't feel like it." Maybe Jesus was ministering far away. Maybe she needed to run errands instead. But no! She determined to go, in spite of anything that might have stood in her way.

Sadly, many people who are ailing can't even be bothered to drive to a healing meeting. If the locale where such an event is deemed inconvenient, they can't be bothered to attend, no matter what health issue they are facing.

Anyone can witness and be a missionary to the unsaved world around them. They simply have to obey God.

Everyone has a disability of some kind, though it may not be visible. Once you hear the testimony of a young man with no arms or legs, you have no excuse not to minister to others. People confined to wheelchairs have a good excuse not to travel around the world, but many of them are still going wherever God sends them, despite the inconveniences posed by a wheelchair. Anyone can witness and be a missionary to the unsaved world around them. They simply have to obey God.

Others' Opinions

The woman with the issue of blood encountered further opposition from the disciples who were trying to protect Jesus from the crush of the frantic crowds. Nobody was supposed to get close to Jesus. If somebody penetrated the wall of the Secret Service and accessed the president of the United States, what do you think would happen? The security agents involved would be fired because they had failed to do their job. In this case, however, God turned it into a miracle. As weak as she was, this woman had to penetrate that human barrier. She had an amazing degree of faith. She knew that she was going to get healed. She said to herself, *"If only I may touch His garment, I shall be made well"* (Matthew 9:21).

In Bible times, this woman could have been stoned simply for leaving home to go shopping—doing so in her condition was illegal. Anyone who came within fifty yards of her would have been considered unclean and would have been required to go through a ceremonial cleansing process. She couldn't go into the temple or participate in any other social activities. This woman went beyond the natural laws of her people and culture. It sounds rather strange, but she was willing to risk her life to get healed. She probably figured, *What do I have to lose?*

Are you willing to put your reputation on the line? Would you risk your life to get close to Jesus and receive His healing touch? I am not suggesting that you break the law or violate any established guidance, as God expects all Christians to submit to secular authority in these matters. (See 1 Peter 2:13.) Do not misinterpret what I am saying to you. She simply went beyond all the limits of ceremonial law of Judaism in her day. She was rejected by religion and by man, but she was healed by the Master, all because of her invincible faith.

Doubt and Defeatism

I imagine the woman with the flow of blood was tempted to give up countless times. After all, her doctors had given up on her. If the "professionals" say something can't be fixed, we tend to believe them—especially when twelve years have gone by with no relief in sight. Yet the woman did not lose hope. She exercised faith in the face of overwhelmingly negative circumstances.

If something is going sideways in your life today, what started it? You can listen to negative people who say, "You must have committed a sin!" Such was the case for a man blind from birth, whom Jesus healed. The disciples asked Jesus, *"Rabbi, who sinned, this man or his parents, that he was born blind?"* (John 9:2). Similarly, the "friends" of Job asked him, when his family had been killed and his resources obliterated, *"If your sons have sinned against Him, He has cast them away for their transgression....If you were pure and upright, surely now He would awake for you, and prosper your rightful dwelling place"* (Job 8:4, 6). They mean well, although their words could be received as condemnation instead of encouragement.

Yes, you must examine yourself. Have you done anything to open the door to this situation? You may not have broken any of the Ten Commandments; however, a simple statement, such as "I always get the flu at this time of year," or "I will probably be a failure, like my father" can open the door to the enemy. You haven't sinned; however, you are in a negative frame of mind and are expecting disaster. Who is the author of disaster? It is the devil, whose goal is *to "steal, and to kill, and to destroy"* (John 10:10). By speaking doubt and defeat instead of determined faith, you invite the devil into your circumstances.

By speaking doubt and defeat instead of determined faith, you invite the devil into your circumstances.

At a recent service, a woman told me that her doctors had said she would be better off dead. I would change doctors if mine had given me that kind of "counsel." I would find someone to speak positive words over me, not a death sentence.

You must determine to dwell on the promises of God if you expect to receive a miracle. Is your glass half full or half empty? Are you a positive person who looks for the good in life and greets each day with a smile? Perhaps you always see the negative side and expect the worst. Guess what? You will get what you expect! Remember, *"Whatever a man sows, that he will also reap"* (Galatians 6:7), and *"As [a man] thinks in his heart, so is he"* (Proverbs 23:7).

As you think, so you are. What you surround yourself with, you will become. How you see yourself, so you will be. Don't be a garbage container. Be the salt of the earth and the light of the world. Let His Word shine through You. Let Jesus work through you as you reach out to touch someone else. Let your miracle be a welcoming beacon to the next person trying to claw their way out of poverty, sickness, and bondage.

Receiving your miracle is your choice. Do you want to stay healed in all areas of your life? Well, you have some work to do. What do you think of first thing in the morning? It is your choice. You can praise God for another beautiful day, or you can start complaining about another busy hectic day. You can thank Him for your wonderful husband and family, or complain about the mess they left in the kitchen the night before. Praise Him that you have family to enjoy and care for instead of the alternative—being alone with no one to love.

Praising God drives the enemy crazy. Not only that, your praise and adoration drive the enemy right out of your home, your car, and your presence. Praising God brings Him into every situation, no matter where you are. The devil can't stand to be in the presence of God. He and his demons will disappear into darkness at the sound of the precious name of Jesus.

Every time I wake up, I want the devil to say, "Watch out—she's awake again!" Sleeping or waking, I know that I know God's angels are surrounding me with His protection. If I am in His will and being obedient to Him, I am within His protection every minute of my life, and that knowledge gives me boldness to expect my miracles.

Face Down Your Fears

What is keeping you from your miraculous blessings? What things in your life are keeping you from doing all that God has called you to do?

Maybe you are experiencing an assault in the area of your finances. God is releasing many of you from those attacks, even though you are struggling now. But you have to keep giving. You have to keep pressing on. You have to keep moving forward and not fall away, because that's exactly what the devil wants you to do. He does not want you to be blessed. He does not want you to live for

God. He certainly doesn't want you to give money to advance God's kingdom and promote His glory. Typically, when people are under financial attack, the first area in which they cut back is their contributions to the church, through tithes and offerings. Yet that is the last thing a believer should do when faced with a financial crisis.

What price are you willing to pay for the call of God on your life? What are you willing to sacrifice to walk out and fulfill the will of God for your life? Do you believe God will supply provision for all He has created and called you to do? If so, then take the next step!

Determine to See Others Healed and Made Whole

The faith of the woman with the issue of blood was an inspiration to those around her. It says in Luke 8:47 that upon being healed, the woman *"declared to* [Jesus] *in the presence of all the people the reason she had touched Him and how she was healed immediately."* What a witness!

You have the ability to tell others Jesus will heal them if they come to Him believing.

You have the ability to tell others Jesus will heal them if they come to Him believing. If you don't want to lay hands on them right then, you have the ability to invite them to a place where they can be healed. What if the person says no? Well, what if he or she says yes? If they say no, simply shake it off! It is your job to share the truth in love and leave the results to God. How others receive the truth is not your responsibility. Your responsibility is to obey God and trust him to carry out his Word.

Get Your Feet Wet

I am originally from Florida, and I love to walk along the beach and watch the waves roll in from the sea. As you wade in the ocean, the water gets progressively deeper. I remember taking a small child out into the sea for the first time. He had never seen a wave before, and he was afraid. But once he learned what the waves could and could not do, he loved to jump into them and play at the beach fearlessly. But he had to get his feet wet in order to conquer his fear.

Abraham had to be willing to sacrifice his son Isaac, who was the fulfillment of God's covenant promise. Isaac had to be laid on the altar for God to do with as He chose. And that is still true for you today. You must be willing to give up what you treasure most—even your very life—as a living sacrifice to God. You must choose to die to self and live for Christ.

> *Anything you willingly give to God, He will multiply and return to you.*

Anything you willingly give to God, He will multiply and return to you. You can give Him your rotten, confused, wandering life. In return, He will gift you with a wonderful, loving, Spirit-filled life on earth and an eternity with Him.

Stand up and get going with the ministry God has given you. Start in your own home, your present environment. People in need are always within reach.

As you walk by faith and get a little closer to the edge of your comfort zone, the waters of conflict and uncertainty may rise up and cause you to become fearful, to the point where you are tempted to turn back and give up. But if you trust in God, you need not fear.

Listen to God, Not Man

Someone may say, "You, in the healing ministry? Who do you think you are?"

A friend of mine intended to go to one of my healing schools. Her friends told her that the healing ministry was of the devil and couldn't be from God. That is not true, but she was thinking to herself, *What am I going to do?* The things of the Spirit were new to her, and the enemy did not want her to lay hands on the sick. The anointing to heal was all over her, and the enemy was trying to keep her from operating in her calling.

God wants His anointing released. Maybe you are thinking, *I want to pray for somebody, but I'm scared, so I'd better not. I know her; she'll tell me no.* Then you want to pray for a man, but "He's too tall." You want to lay hands on him, but he's a man—you feel you can't lay hands on a man.

Those are empty excuses. You have to press through, just as the woman with the issue of blood did. She was determined to get healed. You need to be equally determined to lay hands on the sick and see them recover. You need to have the same determination that God wants to prosper you and bless you beyond your greatest dreams.

You are the head, not the tail; you are above and not beneath. (See Deuteronomy 28:13.) In everything you put your hand to do, you shall prosper. (See Deuteronomy 28:8.) Don't quit. Those who succeed are people who don't quit. Every millionaire is somebody who refused to give up, in spite of seemingly insurmountable challenges. You have to believe that you are not a quitter. You have God's call on your life.

With God, Success Is Sure

When you are God's favorite—and each of His children is His favorite—you can argue with anointed determination and know that God is backing you up all the way. All that matters is knowing that He has "got your back." I know that I am called, appointed, and anointed. You have to know that, too.

In God's realm, there is no such thing as failure. On the earth is another story. Occasionally, we are asked why miracles seem to be flowing more in one area of the world than in another. Sometimes it seems the innocent faith of believers in other nations literally grabs on to the concept of healing, miracles, and blessings—and won't let go. Actually, we witness miracles around the world; however, the people have to be prepared to receive. Once they are healed, people must testify to what has happened. Get a physician's statement as to the changes and healings that God has done.

Pave the Way to Restoration

Scripture doesn't tell us the age of the woman with the flow of blood, but I believe that she was still young enough to have children. Once she was healed, she would have been allowed to return to a normal life, sleep with her husband, and have more children. The Bible doesn't tell us what happened, but I believe that as a result of her physical healing, her life was restored to her, as well.

> *God wants restoration for everyone! He doesn't just want His children well; He wants them whole—in body, as well as in soul and spirit.*

God wants restoration for everyone! He doesn't just want His children well; He wants them whole—in body, as well as in soul and spirit. (See 1 Thessalonians 5:23.) He wants you completely healed, inside and out; forgiven; set free; strong; and going on to a better life. You need to have the same kind of determination that this sick woman had. She did whatever she could do to get to Jesus and receive her healing.

How powerful is your tongue? You can get people to a miracle service to receive ministry. Or, you can share the good news, lay hands on the sick, and see them recover, wherever you may be. You just have to use what God has already given you.

Determination Trumps Distance

A woman in England had a serious issue of excessive bleeding. The doctors wanted to give her a transfusion of six pints of blood because her hemoglobin level was critically low. Without the transfusion, the woman was told, she would be dead and buried within a few days. As I ministered to her on the telephone, Jesus gave her a supernatural blood transfusion. I saw her the following Saturday. She was totally and completely healed. She looked healthy, had lots of energy and a smile on her face because Jesus had touched her. He can heal just as easily with a phone call as He did when someone touched the hem of His garment.

Do you have godly determination? Are you going to stay in God's Word? Will you faithfully search and study to receive all God has for you? Is your heart and mind open to receive God's love and blessings? Are your arms raised and hands open to claim the blessings as they pass by? God's miraculous blessings are around you all the time—you just have to reach out and catch them. Claim them as yours and put them to work for the kingdom. His blessings are bountiful and abundant. They will overtake you. Recognize them and rejoice as you share them with others!

You Can Do It!

If you are sufficiently determined, you can always get where you need to go. You can get there if you want it badly enough. If you are a "no matter what" kind of person, you will reach your goal. You've got to know that if you get out of bed, you can and will reach and receive a blessing from Jesus. As simple as that sounds, you have to be determined to turn your back on what was and reach for what can be, no matter how busy or tired you are.

You get up and go to work every day. You should be more committed to your church and to God than to your job. Your job is merely temporary, no matter how much money you make or how much you love what you do. However, the people and the ministry of God are eternal, and there is a huge difference between the two.

Our Greatest Example of Determination

We have the greatest example of godly determination in our heavenly Father and His Son, Jesus Christ. God exercised determination when He created the heavens and the earth, in that He made a choice to follow through to the chosen goal, no matter what obstacles He faced. The same was true when He created mankind. In His omnipresence and omniscience, God certainly knew that His kids were going to be tempted by the devil and even succumb to unbelief, confusion, and rebellion along their paths through life. In His infinite wisdom, He knew He was going to be busy taking care of each and every child born on earth. He was and is determined to care for and guide His children in the way they should go in order to live forever with Him in heaven. He was determined to make a way for them to overcome Satan and to inherit eternal life, at the expense of His own Son's life.

If you are designed just like your Father, you contain His DNA—His characteristics—and you can act like Him; you are capable of the same determination that God exhibits. You can pray, seek His wisdom, accept that you have the mind of Christ, and do exactly what your Father wants you to do every day.

Pray with me now:

Father, thank You for Your strength and determination. Help me keep my eyes on the goal, not the distracting circumstances that surround me. I have the mind of Christ and will draw on Your wisdom for every decision I make. Thank You, Jesus. Amen.

8

HAVE A HEART
OF GRATITUDE

*"When [Jesus] had come down from the mountain, great multitudes
followed Him. And behold, a leper came and worshipped Him,
saying, 'Lord, if You are willing, You can make me clean.'
Then Jesus put out His hand and touched him, saying, 'I am willing;
be cleansed.' Immediately his leprosy was cleansed."*
—Matthew 8:1

Few Christians today appreciate the power in praising God and expressing thanks to Him. The Bible is full of expressions of praise, in the Old and New Testament alike. Great things happened when the people praised God: enemies were scattered; people were healed; battles were won. Great books have been written on praise and how vital it is to the believer. The practice of praise is truly life to our souls. We are a people of whom God says, "*I formed* [them] *for myself that they may proclaim my praise*" (Isaiah 43:21 NIV).

Notice what the leper in Matthew 8:1 did when he met Jesus—he fell down and worshipped Him. He praised Jesus before ever asking or expecting Jesus to do anything for him, even though his desperation to be healed must have been great. In Bible times, those with leprosy were outcasts among society. Everyone ran from them, screaming in terror. There was no cure; no hope of being welcomed back into the presence of family or friends. Lepers were tormented, even when they were digging in the garbage for tidbits of food discarded by others. Children threw stones at them, and adults cursed them. Yet this man's first response to meeting Jesus was not complaining or pleading but praising.

Whatever happened to praise and worship in the early church? A religious spirit took over and insisted that everyone had to be quiet, pray silently, sing sweetly, and refrain from showing excitement. The power of real worship was turned off. The power source was cut, so to speak.

> *When you get your mind off your problems and onto Jesus, you put yourself in a position to receive from God.*

Years ago, someone made a comment that really spoke to me: "Praise is the plow that makes the furrow in our heart to prepare it to receive from God." This is the reason why our church, along with many others, begins every healing service with a time of praise and worship. When you get your mind off your problems and onto Jesus, you put yourself in a position to receive from God. As long as you keep dwelling on your problems and your illnesses, you haven't turned on the switch to

God's power. You have blocked the flow of the Spirit. You have dammed up the rivers of living water that want to flow through your innermost being.

Greed Versus Gratitude

Very early in life, children learn to say, "Mine." They reach out to take whatever they please, and they throw a tantrum if they don't get it immediately. Years later, after consistent correction, a child learns to share and, finally, to give. Giving with pleasure and joy is an advanced lesson in life. In fact, some people never learn to receive or to give with a godly attitude.

Children who never learn to give or share tend to "take" whatever they want, whenever they want it. They believe that everything and everyone exists for their personal use or abuse. People who take possessions from others without permission are called thieves and can be prosecuted and punished. They are not "receiving"; they are taking. There is a big difference.

Be Open and Ready to Receive

To me, the act of receiving implies a willingness to accept whatever is given with a smile and a grateful heart. You have to be open and expectant in order to truly receive all that God has prepared for you. As His child, you should stand with open arms stretched toward heaven, ready to receive the showers of His blessings. If you stand with your arms locked over your chest and a grumpy expression on your face, insisting, "I don't need anyone or anything; I can do everything by myself," you aren't in a position to receive anything from anyone. People will shy away from you. Children may run. Only the brave will approach you, cautiously, expecting a verbal and/or physical explosion on account of your unpleasant and unwelcoming appearance.

Ask, Don't Demand

Demanding things from people doesn't work very well. Demanding things from God doesn't work, either. He is not your servant. Your children cannot and should not demand you to take care of them and provide them with all their whims. Neither is your Father in heaven going to respond to whines and demands. He responds to a grateful heart of obedience and faith.

If your children finish their homework, clean their rooms, assist with dinner, and complete their chores, how will you respond if they ask you for something? You will probably be more receptive to their requests, and more likely to grant them, than if your children did not finish their homework, refused to complete their chores, and treated others rudely. And you would probably go out of your way to grant their requests if they maintain a positive attitude while performing their chores, rather than reserving their polite manners and sweet smile for those times when they want something from you.

Unfortunately, all of God's kids forget the rules outlined in His Word from time to time. They forget their manners and jump to the "demanding" stage, and then they wonder why God doesn't respond immediately to their selfish demands! Years ago, I saw a wall hanging bearing this phrase: "Nothing improves My hearing like praise." That truly was God speaking. He responds to praise and worship much more readily than to grumpy attitudes and whiny demands.

Give Thanks

Giving gifts is especially joyful when the recipient is grateful. Those who show appreciation for the gifts you give them increase the likelihood of your extending the same generosity in the future. On the other hand, if the recipient scoffs at your gift or makes fun of the gesture, you'll be in no hurry to give him another gift. Remember the laughs and giggles, the joy and exuberance, of a child who opens a present to discover their most wanted toy at Christmas. A doll, a train, a wagon, or bicycle can excite a child's imagination for thousands of hours. He will treasure not only the gift but also the memories.

Our God is no different. He loves to give gifts to His children. He has storehouses full of treasure for each and every child of the King. He loves to make you smile. What does He want in return? The same thing you expect from your own children in return for your gifts to them: love, devotion, praise, adoration, and appreciation.

The Blessings of Gratitude

Praise is a great way to express your gratitude to God. In fact, the benefits of this practice far exceed those of the gift for which you are thanking Him!

Praise Ushers You into God's Presence

But let the [uncompromisingly] righteous be glad; let them be in high spirits and glory before God, yes, let them [jubilantly] rejoice! Sing to God, sing praises to His name, cast up a highway for Him who rides through the deserts—His name is the Lord—be in high spirits and glory before Him!
(Psalm 68:3–4 AMP)

The praises of the righteous create a highway, a pathway for God. You open yourself to Him, allowing Him to work in and through you along that highway of praise. As you praise Him, your spirit will rise. Praise opens the door to His throne room and gives you permission to enter into His presence with thanksgiving.

> *God's name means everything. To the believer, just the mention of His name should bring forth praise and worship.*

David exhorts us to sing praises to His name. Why? Because His name alone encompasses all that He is. God's name means everything. To the believer, just the mention of His name should bring forth praise and worship.

Once you learn to prepare for God in the right way, following His instructions, you will never think that church is dull or unexciting. When your heart is furrowed by praise before you even enter the building, the praise of the worship service may cause your spirit to float right through the ceiling.

Praise Creates an Atmosphere for Miracles

During a Healing Explosion in Bogotá, Colombia, many years ago, we had one of the most glorious praise and worship services ever, with incredible miracles occurring. People were healed, delivered, and set free while the believers there sang their praise and worship to God. Men, women, and children came out of wheelchairs and were walking around the large arena, praising God. An older gentleman received his sight and wandered all over in total amazement as he praised God for his glorious healing.

Throughout the Bible, the people of God found victory when they praised Him. Whether going around Jericho seven times or raising His standard before a battle with the enemy, God and His angels were the protection for the children of Israel. When His kids were obedient, they lived in peace and tranquility. When they acted out in disobedience, they were led away captive and enslaved.

It is no different today. If you are obedient to God's Word, and if you do what He says instead of going your own way, He is there to guide you along the right path. Sometimes the path may be rocky and rough, but when He is guiding you, your destiny can be nothing less than victory. God wins every battle. As His soldier, you just have to line up behind Him. He is the Five-Star General who commands His troops. You simply stand at attention, listen closely, and obey.

Praise Puts the Enemy to Flight

> *Praise drives the enemy right out the door, because he can't stand to listen to the exaltation of the Lord.*

There is nothing in the whole world that will bring joy, rest, peace, trust, hope, expectation, faith, healing, and love more rapidly than the praise of God. Praise drives the enemy right out the door, because he can't stand to listen to the exaltation of the Lord. So, sing your favorite praise song! In fact, you may recognize many Scripture verses as exactly that—one of your favorite praise songs. Many of the Psalms so beautifully express thanks to God that hundreds of verses from that book have been set to music and are used around the world, daily, in praise and worship of our heavenly Father.

Just start praising and thanking God for all the great and mighty things He has done in the past. Praise can be compared to saying, "Thank you," and it is very important to God. After all, it is mentioned approximately 500 times in the Bible. You can be sure that praise is key to a victorious Christian life.

Praise Fuels Your Faith for Miracles

When a real disaster surrounds you, you can barely muster a thought of praise, let alone start speaking or singing anything aloud. Yet belief is necessary for the manifestation of our miracles.

But without faith it is impossible to please Him, for he who comes to God must believe that He is, and that He is a rewarder of those who diligently seek Him. (Hebrews 11:6)

But let him ask in faith, with no doubting, for he who doubts is like a wave of the sea driven and tossed by the wind. For let not that man suppose that he will receive anything from the Lord; he is a double-minded man, unstable in all his ways. (James 1:6–8)

Many, O Lord my God, are Your wonderful works which You have done; and Your thoughts toward us cannot be recounted to You in order; if I would declare and speak of them, they are more than can be numbered. (Psalm 40:5)

What better way to build your faith than to remember all of the wonderful things God has done for you and your loved ones, and to thank Him for those things? Sharing what God has done not only builds your faith to face your present circumstances; it also enables you to be a bold witness for others who are undoubtedly watching to see how you will react in times of pressure.

I share testimonies of healings and miracles witnessed by the ministry team during every meeting, at lunch, on the phone—wherever I am. Why? Because it is exciting to see what God is doing, and I have to share it with others. Hearing about His works builds faith for the next miracle. Talking about what we have seen and heard is scriptural. We are giving God glory every time we share His miracles with another person. We are instructed—no, we are commanded—to tell everyone about our great and glorious God and what He is doing on the earth. (See, for example, Ephesians 5:19–20.)

Echoing the Psalmist

At those times when you need that extra boost of faith, the easiest way to praise God is to read the expressions of praise found in the Psalms. When you need God's power to do a work within you, whether healing, peace, love, joy, or something else—in times of distress, unrest, unhappiness, doubt, and misery—read these verses of praise to Him. Better yet, read them out loud, so that your eyes see them, your lips pronounce them, your ears hear them, and your mind understands them. Your faith will explode as you gain the revelation of this weapon at your disposal—the weapon of praising God.

> *But thou art holy, O thou that inhabitest the praises of Israel.*
>
> (Psalm 22:3 KJV)

According to Scripture, God literally inhabits your praises. How important it is to praise God! It's almost as if you give Him life by speaking forth your thanks. Forget "almost"—you really do give Him life when you surrender yourself to Him for His use: your voice to speak, your hands to reach, your heart to love. Praising God ushers you right into His throne room, where He can give you directions—messages right from His heart. When you need God right in your midst, all you have to do is praise His name with all your heart. God can't resist your praises, because praise was the reason you were created. It says in Psalm 102:18 (KJV), "*This shall be written for the generation to come: and the people which shall be created shall praise the LORD.*"

When you need God right in your midst, all you have to do is praise His name with all your heart.

A great way to begin is with Psalm 103, which provides an excellent summary of your reasons for praising God. I encourage you to open your Bible now and read aloud this wonderful expression of praise. Let your spirit absorb every blessed word as you glean God's strength from each verse. Feel His power flow through you. Let your faith arise from your innermost being. Let your praises "plow furrows" in your heart of stone, making it a heart of flesh open and fertile to receive God's healing power and utter love.

Praise Him for the New Song of Salvation

> *He has put a new song in my mouth; praise to our God; many will see it and fear, and will trust in the LORD.* (Psalm 40:3)

God certainly gave me a new song when I accepted Him into my heart. He also gave my mom, Frances Hunter, a new song. Before she got saved, she was a wild sinner. She drank, she smoked, and she was the life of every party, because she knew more dirty jokes than anyone else. When she got saved, she told God, "I'll give You all of me if You will give me all of You."

A few short weeks after Mom came to salvation, I followed. She asked me what it was that had convinced me to accept Jesus, and I told her, "I saw what a drastic change He made in your life."

Almost overnight, everything about my mother changed. Watching the miraculous transformation in my mother made a life-changing impression on me. I knew that something wonderful happened to her. I witnessed her new life and new song, and I wanted the same thing in my life. In no time at all, had God rearranged both our lives and set us on His path.

No one could deny the new song, the new desires, and the new love for Jesus that Mom had. The one thing He didn't change was her boldness. He used it. Once she started talking about Him, she never stopped. She trusted Him and relied on Him every day of her life.

Praise Him for His Righteousness

I will praise the LORD according to His righteousness, and will sing praise to the name of the LORD Most High. (Psalm 7:17)

God is truly good, always guiding you on the right path, the road of mercy and justice. He deserves to be praised. You are blessed as you lift your voice to Him with songs of joy and thanksgiving.

Praise Him for His Marvelous Works

I will praise You, O LORD, with my whole heart; I will tell of all Your marvelous works. I will be glad and rejoice in You; I will sing praise to Your name, O Most High. (Psalm 9:1–2)

God doesn't stop with just one or two blessings; He pours them out on you every day. What joy can be found in recognizing those blessings and in praising Him for what He has done! Try making a list of the ways in which God has blessed you. I think you will find yourself buying a new notebook every week.

> *Sing praises to the LORD, who dwells in Zion! Declare His deeds among the people.* (Psalm 9:11)

God is truly good, always guiding you on the right path, the road of mercy and justice. He deserves to be praised.

Witness, witness, witness! Tell others what God has done for you! Make a list of all His accomplishments in your life. Go on with a list of good things He has done in your family's lives and then go on to your friends' lives. Thank Him; sing His praise for every item on that list. Call three friends and tell them all the things God has done for you. Declare His doings among the people. Give others an encouraging message of good news they can share with everyone they talk to. Your miracles will multiply and ripple across the environment of friends that surround you.

Praise Him for His Protection

> *"For the oppression of the poor, for the sighing of the needy, now I will arise," says the LORD; "I will set him in the safety for which he yearns."* (Psalm 12:5)

How often you have trusted, leaned on, and been confident in God's mercy and loving-kindness! Your heart should rejoice every time you think of what He has done for you. Who else takes care of you so willingly and unconditionally? Who else supplies you with everything you need? Who else is always there for you? Allow your heart to rejoice and your spirit rise into the clouds with praise for all that He is, for all that He's done, and for all that He has given you.

Praise Him for His Nearness

> *The LORD is near to all who call upon Him, to all who call upon Him in truth.* (Psalm 145:18)

When you have a need that only He can meet, praise Him! Give Him your life through your praise and worship! Invite Him into your circumstances!

Praise Him Publicly

I will declare Your name to My brethren; in the midst of the assembly I will praise You. (Psalm 22:22)

I will give You thanks in the great assembly; I will praise You among many people. (Psalm 35:18)

David was boldly sharing God's praises with others around him. He wasn't quietly religious about what God had done for Him. David is described as a man after God's own heart. (See 1 Samuel 13:14; Acts 13:22.) Obviously, David's praise was well received in heaven's ears. Shouldn't yours be the same?

Praise Him Continually

I will bless the LORD at all times; His praise shall continually be in my mouth. (Psalm 34:1)

Let me ask a question: Can you praise God and complain about your problems at the same time? Can you gossip and witness at the same time? Of course not. God tells you to bless the Lord at all times—to keep His praise continually in your mouth. In this instruction is found the secret to keeping your heart and mind clean and free from sin. If you keep your mind on Him and what He has done for you, others will notice and soon find themselves desiring what you have found. They know you have problems, just like they do, but it is how you handle them that makes the difference. Instead of filling your mind with anxiety and worry, praise God as He solves your problems and brings about the perfect solutions.

You must give thanks to God everywhere you go. Psalm 34:1 doesn't say to praise God just among the saved, the believers, does it? Do you think God is telling you that you must praise Him even in the midst of unbelievers? In the grocery store? At school? In the airport? Oh yes, praise His holy name everywhere! Say, "Praise God!" right where you are. Shout, "Hallelujah! Praise God!"

Praise Him for Granting Access to His Courts

Enter into His gates with thanksgiving, and into His courts with praise. Be thankful to Him, and bless His name. (Psalm 100:4)

Entering His gates on the way to church with thanksgiving prepares hearts to hear God's message from the pastor that day. The gates don't have to mean the entrance of the parking lot to the church. The "gates" can be the car doors as everyone enters the vehicle, they can be the prayer at the breakfast table, or perhaps they can be the moment you wake up in the morning. The "gates" represent the time you have chosen to prepare yourself to receive from God. If you want to receive from God any day of the week, you would prepare the same way, wouldn't you?

When you are prepared coming through the "gates," then you can enter into His courts with praise. His courts are one step closer to His presence, His throne room. When you are praising Him, thanking Him for His good works and blessing His name, all the problems of daily life seem to float away. The pressures of the world suddenly become unimportant as you become surrounded by His being—His joy, His faithfulness, His mercy, and His perfect love.

Psalm 100:4 is key to an important aspect of ministry. You are to enter into His gates with thanksgiving. Does thanksgiving include discussing problems with the kids? No! Does it include discussing where to eat after church? No! Does it include remembering all the things God has provided for the family during the week? Absolutely! Does it mean thanking Him for healing a sore back Tuesday evening or allowing you to witness to an unsaved neighbor in the middle of cutting the grass on Saturday morning? Of course!

Praise Him for Prospering and Beautifying His People

For the LORD takes pleasure in His people; He will beautify the humble with salvation. (Psalm 149:4)

God doesn't only *"take pleasure"* in the humble; He beautifies them with salvation. We have often noticed the physical changes that occur when a person gets saved, healed, or delivered. All these things are possible when believers are praising and worshipping God! The furrowed brow smoothes and relaxes, the eyes sparkle, and a smile breaks the frown. God pours out victory over the oppressed and sets them free! Of course, they will look different. They will be at peace. They will be surrounded with joy—His joy!

Praise Him Early

It is good to give thanks to the LORD, *and to sing praises to Your name, O Most High; to declare Your lovingkindness in the morning, and Your faithfulness every night.* (Psalm 92:1–2)

David rose up early in the morning with God's praise on his lips. What an example! Do you rise early in the morning to praise God? If you got out of bed in the morning praising God for His love and thanking Him for His faithfulness in keeping you safe during your sleeping hours, wouldn't your entire day be easier? God gives you directions in the first waking hours, when your mind is unclouded with the clutter of the day. Look forward to God's alarm clock every morning and His directions for your new day. You will find delight in giving thanks to the Lord when you have His direction from your first waking hour until the last of the day.

> *If you start every day by giving God praise for what He has done and what He is going to do for you, the day will go better for you.*

If you start every day by giving God praise for what He has done and what He is going to do for you, the day will go better for you. Miracles will overtake you. Your channel to God will be open from daybreak, allowing Him access to work in you and through you all day long. And some people say Christians don't have any fun! They don't know what they are missing.

Praise Him in Singing

Make a joyful shout to God, all the earth! Sing out the honor of His name; make His praise glorious.   (Psalm 66:1–2)

Make a joyful noise unto the LORD, all the earth: make a loud noise, and rejoice, and sing praise.   (Psalm 98:4 KJV)

> *Your praises are like laughter in Satan's face, causing him to cower and crawl away to his hiding place in utter defeat.*

God has a sense of humor, doesn't He? His Word tells you to make a joyful noise! He doesn't give you rules of harmony and perfect pitch. He accepts your expressions of joyful gratitude, regardless of the form in which you prefer to make them. So, sing forth with all your heart! God hears only praise; He does not pay attention to pitch, perfect harmony, or tone quality.

He wants you to serve Him gladly and joyfully. He plainly says you are to come before His presence with singing! Make a joyful noise! Sing! Rejoice while you work for Him! Praise Him and enter into His presence, right where you are at this moment!

Your praises are like laughter in Satan's face, causing him to cower and crawl away to his hiding place in utter defeat. Do you have to be big or little? Loud or soft? Young or old? Praise is just as effective from a small child as it is from a mature adult! And praise songs sung quietly are just as powerful as loud rejoicing and forceful clapping. Praise and worship in every form is pure power to God's people!

Praise Him with Music

My heart is steadfast, O God, my heart is steadfast; I will sing and give praise. Awake, my glory! Awake, lute and harp! I will awaken the dawn.

(Psalm 57:7–8)

Also with the lute I will praise You—and Your faithfulness, O my God! To You I will sing with the harp, O Holy One of Israel. My lips shall greatly rejoice when I sing to You, and my soul, which You have redeemed.

(Psalm 71:22–23)

David's joy was overflowing in these psalms. I can just hear him searching for more and more ways to praise God.

Some people claim that musical instruments should not be used in church. I say, play the harp! Play the lyre! Shout for joy! Somehow, I can't imagine David praising God quietly in a corner of his kingdom with his head bowed in silence. He shouted! He danced! His innermost being shouted with joy to God!

Praise Him Spontaneously

To You belongs silence (the submissive wonder of reverence which bursts forth into praise) and praise is due and fitting to You, O God, in Zion; and to You shall the vow be performed. (Psalm 65:1 AMP)

Have you ever been so appreciative of something that someone has done for you that you were nearly bursting before you could express your thanks? Have you ever been so happy that the joy just burst forth from within you without containment? Of course, you have. We all have, from time to time. As a young child, perhaps it was for a special gift that your heart longed for such as a train, a doll, or a puppy. As a teenager, your first kiss propelled you to the heights. On your wedding day, and upon the birth of your first child, you must have felt utter, joyful abandon.

Is there any wonder that many cry in the mere presence of God? To experience Him in reverence and awe and wonder brings forth praise in everyone. In His presence, praise bursts forth spontaneously. Who should be praised more than God, who always keeps His promises to take care of His children?

David's innermost being shouted God's praises, as well as his lips. Imagine the complete joy that overtook David when he thought of God's goodness, power, and love.

Can you remember that first feeling of total joy when you knew that you knew that you knew that Jesus had saved you and now lived within you? Do you recall the overflowing joy when God first healed you or a loved one? Meditate on how you felt the very first time you truly experienced God's love and presence.

Praise Him for His Constant Presence

God is omnipresent, meaning He is everywhere at all times. You really can't get away from Him. He is always within reach, although rebellious behavior and other forms of disobedience cloud His presence, preventing you from sensing Him. Yet your songs of rejoicing will open your heart, awaken your mind, and attune your ears to His presence. Worship causes the "cloud" to vanish and increases your sensitivity to recognize His presence. The communication channel opens again, so that you can again "feel" Him and His anointing.

Praise Him for His Righteous Judgment

> *Let the peoples praise You, O God; let all the peoples praise You. Oh, let the nations be glad and sing for joy! For You shall judge the people righteously, and govern the nations on earth. Let the peoples praise You, O God; let all the peoples praise You.* (Psalm 67:3–5)

David has turned from his emphasis on personal concerns at this point. He is asking God to let all the people of the earth experience His joy and sing praises to Him because they had found the same guidance, understanding, mercy, and fair judgment that David had found from God. He knew that God would treat everyone with that same mercy and wisdom. David wanted to share that overwhelming joy with everyone. You can do the same, can't you?

Praise Him for His Wonderful Creation

> *Let heaven and earth praise Him, the seas and everything that moves in them.* (Psalm 69:34)

Once I discovered the wonders of God's creation, and once it was revealed to me what He had done to redeem it, I received a new outlook on the world around me. Everything within the universe truly was created to praise God.

Who could deny the beauty of a tree with its branches reaching up to heaven? Who could deny the magnificent intricacies of the human body and the complex ways in which it functions? When you consider the heavens with its sun, moon, and stars, can you deny the beauty, power, and wisdom of the One who created them? All of God's creations and the balance of life are breathtaking. All of creation declares His praise!

Praise Him for Never Failing You

For You are my hope, O Lord GOD; You are my trust from my youth; by You I have been upheld from birth; You are He who took me out of my mother's womb. My praise shall be continually of You. I have become as a wonder to many, but You are my strong refuge. (Psalm 71:5–7)

Man may fail us, but God is completely trustworthy. He never changes. He took me from birth and looked after me. He guided me and loves me, in spite of my shortcomings and problems. Yes, I can say I am *"as a wonder."* There are people from my past who would never recognize me today. They would have a hard time believing what God has done to me ever since I allowed Him to take over my entire life. God is my refuge. He has become my teacher! I love every day with Him! I was nothing without Him! Now, He has my back!

Let All the Earth Praise Him

If you ever feel like you're the only one who wants to thank God for what He has done, just listen for the angels—they speak His praises all day long and will join you in your glorious praise! The angelic hosts worship Him just for who He is, not for what He's done for them. The angels don't need His faithfulness like you do. So, shouldn't you praise Him even more than they? Shouldn't you worship Him just for who He is?

Therefore by Him let us continually offer the sacrifice of praise to God, that is, the fruit of our lips, giving thanks to His name.

(Hebrews 13:15)

God doesn't "need" your praise. He knows how important it is for you to offer it to Him, even if it truly becomes a "sacrifice of praise"—when you don't feel like rejoicing. (See Jeremiah 33:11.) Oh, how important praise is to God! How important praise and worship are to the believer! Enter His gates with thanksgiving in your heart! Enter His courts with praise! Bless His name! Bask in His presence and receive His strength!

Psalm 148 orders praise from everything everywhere, not just man. Literally everything He has created is to praise Him and exalt His name. Is there any question who or what should be praising Him? Do you have to wait until you are in a church building? A thousand times, no! You are to praise Him everywhere you are. And everything on earth and in the heavens is to praise Him.

Here's something you may not have known—God sings over *you*! It says in Zephaniah 3:17, "*The* LORD *your God in your midst, the Mighty One, will save; He will rejoice over you with gladness, He will quiet you with His love, He will rejoice over you with singing.*" God rejoices over His children. He blesses His kids! Are you one of His children? Praise God! I want to curl up right next to Him, don't you? I want to hear Him sing praises to me and you! Through those praises, there is power and prosperity! Do you need His power? His prosperity? Oh, yes! In order to spread His Word, to show His miracles, to reach out to the hurting unsaved, you indeed need His power and prosperity! In yourself, you are and can do nothing; but with Him, you can move mountains! (See Matthew 17:20; 21:21; Mark 11:23.)

> *Praise is vital to every area of your life! The more you praise God, the more power He will pour out on you and through you.*

Is there really any question that there is power in praise? Praise is vital to every area of your life! The more you praise God, the more power He will pour out on you and through you. I want His power! I will praise Him all day long! I will worship Him with everything in me!

Release that power from deep inside of your spirit. Keep on thanking Him! Keep on praising Him, and don't let up. I can't fully explain what happens inside of you, but when it happens, you will know that God's power is within you and is bursting forth from every cell of your body. Then, joy will rise up within you! Peace will overtake you! Healing will manifest itself! People around you will wonder what happened to you! Your appearance will change! The joy of the Lord will cover you and take the burdens away! Opportunities to witness will knock on your door! Watch God work as He takes pleasure in your praises. Soon you will have even more reasons to praise Him!

Stay in His perfect will for your life. You will be positioned to receive His blessings. You will be open to be obedient to His still small voice and be ready to follow his instructions. You will receive more and more revelation. You will not just be a receptacle but a deliverer. His blessings will flow through you. You will deliver His blessings, His Word, His freedom, and His healing power to the next person who is searching for what you have found.

As you praise, you will receive the blessings of God; and as you continue to praise Him in thanksgiving, you will maintain your blessings. The cycle will continue as long as you keep on praising God and recognizing His blessings! That's why you must echo the psalmist and say, "O LORD my God, I will give thanks to You forever" (Psalm 30:12). Keep on thanking Him! Lift up an unceasing song of grateful worship to the One who alone is worthy, and you will never lose your joy at the miracles He sends your way.

Let's pray!

Heavenly Father, remind me of all Your glorious works. Father, I want Your praises on my lips continually. When I am praising You, I can't be complaining or listening to the enemy's lies. I want an undivided heart that will live only to praise You and listen to Your direction and teaching.

Thank You, Father, for all You've done for me and my family. I am searching for more and more of Your strength, God; for more and more of You. Praising and worshipping You, Father, will keep my mind clear to hear Your direction, to be taught Your ways by the

Holy Spirit, and to allow Jesus to work through me to set the captives free and minister healing and deliverance to the sick.

I praise You, Father, for all the miraculous things You have done. I worship You, Father, just for being You. You are the authority above all things. You are everywhere at all times. I can't fully comprehend everything You are, but I know You are my heavenly Father who wants only the best for me.

I will rise up every morning with Your praises on my lips and walk in faith all day long, Father, guided by You with every step I take, with every word I speak, and with every person I touch.

I praise You, Father, for You are my Lord—You are my everything! I will enter Your gates with thanksgiving every day, Lord! I will enter Your courts with praise and thanksgiving! I will bless Your holy name with my whole being! Thank You, Father! Amen and amen!

PART III:

REMOVING HINDRANCES
TO RECEIVING

9

GET RID OF "DIRTY LAUNDRY"

"Walk as children of light (for the fruit of the Spirit is in all goodness, righteousness, and truth), finding out what is acceptable to the Lord. And have no fellowship with the unfruitful works of darkness."
—Ephesians 5:8–11

Doing the laundry is a lifelong chore. As often as necessary—whether daily, weekly, or monthly—you gather the soiled linens from around the house to be laundered. Some items, such as socks and underwear, you wash on a regular basis. Other items, such as tablecloths and draperies, may require less frequent washes. Under the beds, from the closets, bathroom, kitchen, sports bag, and the laundry basket…wayward items seem to hide in the oddest places sometimes. They may stay hidden for a long time. If a soiled item, such as a sweaty sock, stays out of sight long enough, mold and mildew may take up residence and spread. After a while, the smell will alert you to the fact that something isn't perfect. Hopefully, you are able to locate the item and wash it—or maybe just trash it—before the stench permeates the entire house.

Anyone who walks into that room will know something just isn't right but can't identify the cause. You look around but don't examine every inch. Life is busy; you'll look later. Does it just go away? No, it stays hidden, until you're searching for something nearby and suddenly discover, quite by coincidence, the disgusting mess that is your soiled garment. Now that you are aware of it, you can take care of the mess—clean it up and dispose of it, never to be seen or smelled again.

Sins can be similar. It often happens that you stow away secret sin, forget about it, and neglect to repent or to ask for forgiveness. Perhaps it's because you think that this "little" sin is inconsequential; that God would not withhold any good thing from you on account of such a minor offense.

It's time to get rid of the hidden "dirty laundry" in your life. How do I know about these things? Because everyone—myself included—is faced with the challenge of finding and eliminating whatever is barring God's blessings from our lives.

Years ago, after eighteen years of copastoring a church, I begged God to reveal what was holding back His blessings on the congregation. He was faithful to answer my cry, even though my cries turned to wails at the discovery of my husband's homosexual affairs.

Talk about airing out your "dirty laundry"! Once exposed, this secret sin of his spread everywhere I went. The enemy wanted to destroy every part of my life—my marriage, my home, my children, my church, my friends, and more. In fact, he wanted me dead; he even tried to attach cancer to my body to seal the deal.

The enemy sneaks in so cleverly and subtly to defile a life and discredit a Christian's testimony. That's why it is so important that you ask God daily to reveal any hidden sins in your life. Maybe it is a habit that was developed in childhood. Maybe a thought creeps into your mind from yesteryear to remind you of the carnal things you did before inviting Jesus into your life. You can't afford to let concealed sins block your blessings! When you ask Him, God, through His Holy Spirit, will reveal anything and everything requiring change, and then He will give you the grace to undergo that change.

Eliminating Secret Sins

Sin is anything that defies God and opens the door for the enemy to enter your life—disobedience, rebellion, bitterness, unrighteous anger, unforgiveness, sexual perversion, addiction, alcoholism, and so forth.

Not only does sinful behavior give the devil access to your life; it also ushers in his attacks in the form of diseases to ravage your body.

Not only does sinful behavior give the devil access to your life; it also ushers in his attacks in the form of diseases to ravage your body. Recurring sin, if it is not repented of, puts more and more distance between you and God, until you begin to wonder if He is still present in your life. Each instance of sin is like a layer of fog, accumulating to the point where the cloud blocks your vision, leaving you feeling totally alone. Step by insidious step, you have moved away from Him—His presence, His protection, and His abundant provision for you.

But it doesn't have to be that way. Through confession and repentance, you can turn back to God and return to a position in which you can receive His blessings. When His Holy Spirit came to live within you, you put on the *"new man,"* a process that Paul aptly described in his letter to the church at Ephesus:

But you have not so learned Christ, if indeed you have heard Him and have been taught by Him, as the truth is in Jesus: that you put off, concerning your former conduct, the old man which grows corrupt according to the deceitful lusts, and be renewed in the spirit of your mind, and that you put on the new man which was created according to God, in true righteousness and holiness. (Ephesians 4:20–24)

Cleanse the Heart

Keep your heart with all diligence, for out of it spring the issues of life. (Proverbs 4:23)

Therefore, to him who knows to do good and does not do it, to him it is sin. (James 4:17)

You must keep your heart pure before God if you are to receive His blessings. Bringing every sin to Him through confession and repentance closes the doors through which the enemy would otherwise have access to attack you. It also frees you from sin, so that it no longer has power over you. This step is not a matter of condemnation but of self-examination. God may convict you, but He never condemns you. Sin must be evicted from your life. Recognize it, repent of it, and kick it out!

Prayers for purity are very important. David asked God to cleanse him, not only from known sins, but also from hidden faults:

Who can understand his errors? Cleanse me from secret faults. Keep back Your servant also from presumptuous sins; let them not have dominion over me. Then I shall be blameless, and I shall be innocent of great transgression. (Psalm 19:12–13)

This attitude pleased God, who called David *"a man after My own heart, who will do all My will"* (Acts 13:22). You can follow David's example and pray such psalms as these:

Create in me a clean ["pure" NIV] heart, O God; and renew a right spirit within me. (Psalm 51:10 KJV)

Search me, O God, and know my heart: try me, and know my thoughts: and see if there be any wicked way in me, and lead me in the way everlasting. (Psalm 139:23–24 KJV)

As you invite the Holy Spirit to search your heart, you should be prepared to face some very ugly things—but, praise God, He promises to forget all about them! God says of His children, *"For I will be merciful to their unrighteousness, and their sins and their lawless deeds **I will remember no more"*** (Hebrews 8:12; see also Hebrews 10:17).

Clean Out the Home

The next area you need to purge of Satan's influence is the place where you live. God promises to renew your spirit when you "clean house," according to the following command:

You'll come back and clean house,…throw out all the rotten images and obscene idols. I'll give you a new heart. I'll put a new spirit in you. I'll cut out your stone heart and replace it with a red-blooded, firm-muscled heart. Then you'll obey my statutes and be careful to obey my commands. You'll be my people! I'll be your God! But not those who are self-willed and addicted to their rotten images and obscene idols! I'll see that they're paid in full for what they've done. (Ezekiel 11:18–21 MSG)

Ask God to show you what, if anything, you should remove from your house. The object may have been a gift you received years ago from a friend. Even so, anything with a negative spiritual attachment is not something you want to have hanging around your home.

Your first defense should be to pray over every item that enters your home. Call everything clean and free from anything that could hinder or harm your house or those who live there. Some negative spiritual influences enter subtly, through the avenues of television, computer, radio, and other media outlets. The enemy is cunning and quiet. Anything that disrupts

> *The enemy is cunning and quiet. Anything that disrupts your peace and hampers your relationship with your heavenly Father needs to be dealt with, and quickly.*

your peace and hampers your relationship with your heavenly Father needs to be dealt with, and quickly.

Unwanted spirits can come into your life via coworkers, neighbors, friends, and even family members. Am I telling you to avoid or shun other people? No, just be aware that the enemy sometimes uses other people to get near you and interrupt your walk with God. If a certain individual seems to have a negative influence on your life, you may need to avoid him or her and somehow remove that person from your immediate circle. God must come first.

How can spiritual things attach to objects? Have you ever used a prayer cloth or prayed over one and then given it to someone else? Anointed prayer cloths are used frequently. They are scriptural—the apostle Paul used them, with great effect (see Acts 19:11–12)—and they can be very powerful in sharing the anointing of God. Yet they can also work destruction in the hands of the enemy. Unholy prayers work the same.

Once your house is cleaned, it is your responsibility to keep it free of garbage. By "garbage," I do not mean trash or waste products. The "garbage" I'm talking about consists of the sinful influences that creep in via visitors in your home, as well as through satanic music you may listen to, words of deceit and hatred you may read, inappropriate television programs or Internet content you may see, and so forth.

> But He said, "More than that, blessed are those who hear the word of God and keep it!" (Luke 11:28)

Cast Off Unforgiveness

> For if you forgive men their trespasses, your heavenly Father will also forgive you. But if you do not forgive men their trespasses, neither will your Father forgive your trespasses. (Matthew 6:14–15)

And whenever you stand praying, if you have anything against anyone, forgive him, that your Father in heaven may also forgive you your trespasses. (Mark 11:25)

One of the greatest hindrances to receiving from God is unforgiveness. It shuts the door on heaven's blessings and also hinders prayers. For instance, if a husband and wife are having problems, their prayers won't reach heaven.

Husbands, likewise, dwell with them with understanding, giving honor to the wife, as to the weaker vessel, and as being heirs together of the grace of life, that your prayers may not be hindered. (1 Peter 3:7)

If you are married, I would like to ask you an important question. If Jesus was standing in front of you, would you be rude to Him or argue with Him? Of course not. You would treat Him with utmost respect and honor. If your spouse is a Christian, Jesus lives in him or her, doesn't He? When you look at your spouse, you are looking into the eyes of Jesus. When you touch your spouse, the hand of Jesus living in you is touching the Jesus living in your spouse. If you are looking at your husband or wife—God's gift to you—with anything but loving tenderness, the enemy has deceived you.

> *If you are looking at your husband or wife—God's gift to you—with anything but loving tenderness, the enemy has deceived you.*

Jesus said, "*Where two or three are gathered together in My name, I am there in the midst of them*" (Matthew 18:20). God doesn't say He leaves you or is ignoring you. He is always present, but disagreement and unforgiveness may cloud or even block the blessings He wants to pour all over your marriage. It's your choice whether or not His blessings will flow, so get in agreement and stay there!

Your spouse was probably the best thing that ever happened to you. You believed God chose this person for you and made your vows before Him and earthly witnesses. That same person is still there, though he or she may be hidden by lies from the enemy. Forgive and forget, and love the Jesus in your spouse. Jesus can and will reconcile your relationship. No one person is ever to blame. Usually, the lies have come from both sides. Listen to God's voice and pray for one another. Be open and receive each other's love as if you were young lovers just discovering each other. God will revive your feelings and restore your relationship. He wants to bless your union. Open the windows of heaven and spread your arms wide to receive the blessings He is about to pour over you.

Seek peace. God is a God of peace, love, and order. He is not the author of chaos. Follow peace in every situation, and stay out of unforgiveness and strife.

Division of any kind will weaken a relationship. The saying "divide and conquer" is a strong spiritual truth. There is strength in numbers. God teaches us to come together to pray, share with, and care for one another. We strengthen and encourage one another in God's ways and principles. Alone, we are weak and are easily deceived by lies of the world. Again, God knows best what His children should do to stay healthy within the kingdom.

My husband, Kelley, shared the following two testimonies about unforgiveness.

A lady with serious arthritis came seeking relief from her pain and restricted mobility. After talking to her, deep-seated unforgiveness was uncovered. Prayer to forgive her long-lived hurt and trauma brought remarkable but not complete relief. She was sent home to complete the healing process. Often there are many memories that are not readily brought to mind. As they are remembered, take care of them quickly. Ask for forgiveness.

A person from Tulsa, Oklahoma, came forward for prayer. Nearly every joint was affected by serious arthritic changes. A team member prayed. Nothing happened. The team member prayed again. Nothing happened. Prayer didn't make a difference. Another healing team member ministered further to the person, and it was finally revealed that this individual was harboring unforgiveness toward several people who had caused serious pain in the past. Healing came with forgiveness of those past offenses. Further prayer was not necessary; this healing was directly related to forgiveness.

Keep Yourself from Evil Influences

Therefore we also, since we are surrounded by so great a cloud of witnesses, let us lay aside every weight, and the sin which so easily ensnares us, and let us run with endurance the race that is set before us.

(Hebrews 12:1)

Afterward Jesus found him in the temple, and said to him, "See, you have been made well. Sin no more, lest a worse thing come upon you."

(John 5:14)

Abstain from every form of evil.   (1 Thessalonians 5:22)

As much as you are able, you should stay away from the influences that would weaken your resolve to live holy and pure before the Lord. These influences include people, places, Web sites, movies, and books. For example, recovering alcoholics should steer clear of liquor stores, bars, and restaurants where alcohol is served. They may also be wise to turn down invitations to dinner parties where the forbidden beverages will be consumed.

Similarly, if sexual perversion and/or pornography is a weakness, the person should avoid being alone with a member of the opposite sex. Most pastors I know travel with at least one other person of the same gender, for the sake of accountability. The best thing you can do is remove yourself from the temptation, giving it no chance to entice you.

Correct Your Priorities

A lady came to me for prayer. An accident had mangled her hand and crushed her fingers—she couldn't move them at all. The fingers of one of her hands were held together by several pins, plus bandages. After prayer, her pain decreased to a small degree, and a little mobility was restored to the digits. I continued to pray, but it didn't accomplish anything; her healing progressed no further.

Upon further inquiry, I learned that this lady had suffered the injury while sledding in a part of the country that didn't see snow very often. In her desire to take advantage of the snowy slopes, she skipped church. I led her in a prayer of repentance, in which she asked God to forgive her for disobeying Him by neglecting to be where He wanted her to be. Instantly the pain disappeared and complete mobility was restored to her fingers.

Cultivate Humility, Not Pride

Therefore humble yourselves under the mighty hand of God, that He may exalt you in due time. (1 Peter 5:6)

Pride was the sin that landed Satan in hell. (See Isaiah 14:12–15.) Many people shrug it off, but pride is a big deal to God! Don't believe me? Consider the following Scriptures:

[God says,] "The one who has a haughty look and a proud heart, him I will not endure." (Psalm 101:5)

You [God] rebuke the proud; the cursed, who stray from Your commandments. (Psalm 119:21)

These six things the LORD hates, yes, seven are an abomination to Him: a proud look, a lying tongue, hands that shed innocent blood, a heart that devises wicked plans, feet that are swift in running to evil, a false witness who speaks lies, and one who sows discord among brethren. (Proverbs 6:16–19)

The LORD will destroy the house of the proud. (Proverbs 15:25)

God resists the proud, but gives grace to the humble. (James 4:6; 1 Peter 5:5)

No one with a spirit of pride should expect to receive blessings from God. The good news is, the attitude that's opposite of pride ushers bountiful

blessings into your life! Here is just a sampling of promises to those who live
in a spirit of humility:

> LORD, You have heard the desire of the humble; You will prepare their
> heart; You will cause Your ear to hear.   (Psalm 10:17)

> The LORD lifts up the humble.   (Psalm 147:6)

> For the LORD takes pleasure in His people; He will beautify the humble
> with salvation.   (Psalm 149:4)

> By humility and the fear of the LORD are riches and honor and life.
>   (Proverbs 22:4)

> A man's pride will bring him low, but the humble in spirit will retain
> honor.   (Proverbs 29:23)

> Humble yourselves in the sight of the Lord, and He will lift you up.
>   (James 4:10)

Clearly, there are benefits to being humble. Truly, the spirit of humility gets God's attention! The reason is because in acting, thinking, speaking,
and conducting yourself humbly, you follow the example of God's Son, Jesus
Christ. The epitome of humility, He "humbled Himself and became obedient to
the point of death, even the death of the cross" (Philippians 2:8). And what was the
result of Jesus' humility?

> Therefore [because of Jesus' humble self-sacrifice in dying on the
> cross for our sins] God also has highly exalted Him and given Him the
> name which is above every name, that at the name of Jesus every knee
> should bow, of those in heaven, and of those on earth, and of those under
> the earth, and that every tongue should confess that Jesus Christ is Lord,
> to the glory of God the Father.   (Philippians 2:9–11)

Jesus was exalted to the highest place after humbling Himself to the lowest point. Humility—not pride or arrogance or self-interest—should be your aim! When you follow in the footsteps of Jesus, you get God's attention and trigger an outpouring of His blessings.

> *If I regard iniquity in my heart, the LORD will not hear. But certainly God has heard me; He has attended to the voice of my prayer. Blessed be God, who has not turned away my prayer, nor His mercy from me!*
> (Psalm 66:18–20)

Whom do you hang around? Do you listen to garbage? Are you eating from the wrong table? What you allow to enter is what will exit. The longer you hang around the wrong people and the wrong places, that garbage affects you and your life. Your words change. Your attitude changes. Your faith in God's Word shrinks into a dust ball under the bed in the furthest corner.

The Pure in Heart Will See God

> *Blessed are the pure in heart, for they shall see God.*   (Matthew 5:8)

Stay in righteousness. Hang on to it with tenacious faith. Don't listen to the negative voices from the enemy who wants to destroy you. You are following the Ten Commandments, you say? Great! Keep on going. There is much more to learn. The Ten Commandments are like first grade curriculum—the basics. As you mature toward graduation, much more is expected. Each step of your Christian growth will bring you to a higher level, as long as you learn the lessons and pass the tests.

A young child doesn't recognize dirty laundry piled in a corner or hidden under a bed. He has no idea what the germs can do—no concept of the slow destruction and disintegration of the environment. As an adult or mature Christian, you have to be willing to examine yourself and your environment. You must be ready to *"catch us the foxes, the little foxes that spoil the vines"* (Song of Solomon 2:15). Be ready and prepared to get rid of your dirty laundry! Doing so puts you in a position to receive the miracles and blessings God has in store for you.

10

ESCAPE THE CONFINES OF RELIGION

*"You were not redeemed with corruptible things, like silver or gold,
from your aimless conduct received by tradition from your fathers,
but with the precious blood of Christ, as of a lamb without
blemish and without spot."*
—1 Peter 1:18–19

Wе just talked about the ways in which sinful behaviors can keep you from receiving from God. Many times, you miss God's miracles due to incorrect ways of thinking—ways that are not sinful, per se, but which do not produce the heart of faith that receives from God.

Healing and deliverance were an integral part of Jesus' ministry. Yet somehow, over the centuries, the primary elements of Christian leadership have shifted to teaching, counseling, and administration. Many Christian leaders never pray for the sick because they fear the disbelief and negative reports that may arise among those whose healing does not manifest immediately. These leaders either relegate this area of ministry to others or ignore it completely.

In this way, man-made tradition makes the Word of God ineffective and robs it of relevance to everyday life. As a result, many churches today have been rendered impotent, and they continue to reinforce their own weakness by avoiding the truth and *"making the word of God of no effect"* (Mark 7:13; see also Matthew 15:6), as Jesus convicted the Pharisees and scribes of doing.

When I talk about "religion," I don't mean true Christian faith. Jesus said, *"Pure and undefiled religion before God and the Father is this: to visit orphans and widows in their trouble, and to keep oneself unspotted from the world"* (James 1:27). By "religion," I mean man-made traditions and dry rituals that lack meaning and spiritual significance.

The apostle Paul made a similar point in his letter to the Colossians:

> *If you died with Christ from the basic principles of the world, why, as though living in the world, do you subject yourselves to regulations; "Do not touch, do not taste, do not handle," which all concern things which perish with the using; according to the commandments and doctrines of men? These things indeed have an appearance of wisdom in **self-imposed religion**, false humility, and neglect of the body, but are of no value against the indulgence of the flesh.* (Colossians 2:20–23)

Doubt and Disbelief

The overwhelming majority of Christians have never seen someone miraculously healed. They have never prayed successfully for a healing, nor have they seen anyone else do it. They doubt what they have seen on TV and ignore any testimony reporting any kind of miracle. And when a miracle does manifest, they tell themselves it's merely coincidence or a hysterical reaction.

Yes, for Christians in Western society, God is usually the last resort. When the doctors mention words like "incurable" and "fatal," a churchgoing patient may need to go beyond his own congregation and pastor for prayer. So many people miss out on the healings and miracles available to them, all because they refuse to have faith for such things. They doubt God, selling themselves short in the process.

Christian leaders who prize biblical knowledge above everything else, including supernatural experiences, are amazed when they see young Christians pray for the sick with success. The zeal and excitement of someone newly saved, healed, and set free often overflows as he or she eagerly, and quite successfully, lays hands on the sick and sees miracles and healings. The simple faith of a child can and will bring healing.

Skepticism about miraculous healings is not a new trend. There were skeptics even in Jesus' day. Consider the account previously mentioned under Miracle No. 17, as told in Mark 5:22–24, 35–42, Matthew 9:18–19, 23–26, and Luke 8:41–42, 49–56. Jairus' daughter was at the point of death. He begged Jesus to come to his home and lay hands on her so she would live. Jesus recognized his faith and went with him. He saw all the mourners outside and attempted to reassure them.

[Jesus said,] *"Why make this commotion and weep? The child is not dead, but sleeping." And they ridiculed Him. But when He had put them all outside, He took the father and the mother of the child, and those who were with Him, and entered where the child was lying. Then He took the child by the hand, and said to her, "Talitha, cumi," which is translated, "Little girl, I say to you, arise." Immediately the girl arose and walked, for she was twelve years of age. And they were overcome with great amazement.* (Mark 5:39–42)

All three Gospels in which this story is recorded include the detail that the people laughed when Jesus said that the girl was not dead but asleep. The same thing happens today—people scorn and scoff at any remark concerning the power of God to heal.

We have seen this reaction especially to televised healings. Many viewers laugh when they hear someone say "In Jesus' name" or "Receive your healing, in the name of Jesus." Nothing has changed since Jesus' day. Nor has Jesus Christ; He "*is the same yesterday, today, and forever*" (Hebrews 13:8). The world laughed then, and they still laugh today; but we win! Hallelujah!

Another interesting point in these accounts is that Jesus sent the scoffers away. He had them "put out." (See Matthew 9:25; Mark 5:40; Luke 9:54.) He knew they didn't have the faith necessary to heal the girl. Wouldn't it be wonderful if we had the courage and the boldness today to "put out" anybody who laughed when we were talking about the power of God? If there is an interruption or setback in your miracle, don't give up! Just keep believing it's on the way.

Available to All Believers

> *Experienced or inexperienced, old or young, male or female, all of God's children can be empowered to minister healing to one another, as well as to themselves.*

At the conclusion of every meeting my parents held, my father, Charles Hunter, would minister salvation, followed by the baptism in the Holy Spirit. He would then ask for a volunteer from among the group of newly saved and baptized individuals. Guided by my father's words, the volunteer would lay hands on someone who needed a miracle, and it would manifest. Night after night, this process was a powerful demonstration of the truth that "if Charles and Frances can do it, you can do it, too!" Even young children experienced the joy of allowing God's healing power to flow through their small hands to adults, resulting in the manifestation of a miraculous healing right before their youthful eyes.

Experienced or inexperienced, old or young, male or female, all of God's children can be empowered to minister healing to one another, as well as to themselves. Why don't more people know about this important aspect of ministry? Because they haven't experienced firsthand the power of God to heal.

For many, many years, the church did not teach that healing and miracles were available to believers. The idea of God's power to heal became strange and mysterious. Even the baptism in the Holy Spirit was called "demonic" and considered something to avoid. The supernatural was avoided by mainstream Christians rather than embraced as an everyday reality for the average believer. Christian leaders deliberately ignored this entire facet of Jesus' ministry, and anyone who believed that God's miraculous blessings are available today was laughed at.

Thank goodness some hung on to their beliefs and boldly proclaimed the truth throughout the ages! The Bible is not vague in its teachings on the supernatural, including miraculous healings. You cannot afford to be embarrassed about or selective in your beliefs—nor would you want to! From cover to cover, the Bible is truth. Ask God to open your eyes to the truth—the real truth, in its entirety. The truth is, if you have God's Holy Spirit living within you, greater understanding of the Scriptures is not only possible; it is promised. (See John 16:7, 13–14.)

More than Mere Knowledge

Again, the Christian life must not be confined to mere study of the Bible, resulting in knowledge without application. True Christianity is a wonderful journey—an ongoing experience of the supernatural power of God living and working through you. Daily dependence on God is a necessary element. You will not be trapped in the anti-supernatural theology and/or a non-supernatural lifestyle where you need God only occasionally. You will not avoid places where healing happens. Instead, you will actively search for the exciting moves of God and jump into the middle of it. You will participate, not just observe.

What is religion keeping you from doing? Don't let it rob you of a deep, meaningful relationship with your heavenly Father.

Returning home one day, I talked to a neighbor and said, "I just got back from a miracle service, and it was great!"

"Oh," she replied, "all those people that fall on the floor are actually demon-possessed."

Nothing could be further from the truth! Someone who confuses a miraculous manifestation for demonic possession has never experienced or witnessed the supernatural. When this happens to you, you become so full of the Holy Spirit that you can't even stand. You pass out at the overwhelming greatness of God's presence when He overshadows you and short-circuits your central nervous system. You suddenly find yourself lying peacefully on the floor while God's healing power flows through you.

If you don't have the necessary knowledge to understand this type of experience, you will view it through natural eyes and interpret it with man's limited understanding, and you will never be prepared to receive all the blessings that God has planned for you.

> *Those who argue that illness is intended by God as a means of instruction are drenched in legalism, which deflates the kind of faith necessary to see or experience His miraculous healing power.*

At one time, my children said, "You know, Mom, you should just quit the ministry. You are under such great attack. Just quit."

I will be the first to admit, I have been knocked down a few times. I have run over a few potholes along the way. However, whenever this happens, I just get back up, dust myself off, and keep on going. That is what you are supposed to do. The devil may try to hinder me, and man may trip me up, but I just get up and keep on going. These areas of attack were brought on by others' decisions, not God!

Legalistic Views of Healing

Do you really think it's God's will to heal everyone? Or do you think God afflicts you with sickness in order to "teach you a lesson"? The truth is, God wants to heal each and every one of His children, including you. And He does not send any infirmity, for He gives only good things. Remember, *"Every good gift and every perfect gift is from above, and comes down from the Father of lights, with whom there is no variation or shadow of turning"* (James 1:17).

Those who argue that illness is intended by God as a means of instruction are drenched in legalism, which deflates the kind of faith necessary to see or experience His miraculous healing power.

Incorrect View No. 1: Healing Is Not for Today

I love to tell the story of one of the first big miracles to happen in my parents' early days of ministering. Shortly after they had received the baptism of the Holy Spirit, they went to a church where the people were unaware of this experience. My mother was going to give a brief presentation on how to make the Bible come alive; but, as she and my dad were traveling to the church, God said to them, "I want you to share that healing is for today!"

What a day of miracles it was! One little seventy-year-old lady was bent over with osteoporosis so far that you could not see anything but her back as she slowly made her way down the aisle. They spoke healing to her, and she was slain in the Spirit under the power of God. As she was gently lowered to the floor, there was a tremendous "cracking" sound; and when she stood up, she was inches taller than before! She no longer had a "hump" on her back; she was as straight as an arrow!

She had always sat in the front pew of the church because she was so bent over, she could not fit into any of the other pews. On Sunday morning, she sat in her usual place; this time, however, she was sitting straight up! The pastor's message that morning was entitled "Healing Is Not for Today." Every time he made that statement, she said, "Hallelujah!" He continued, "Healing is of the devil," and she answered, "Hallelujah!" My parents returned to that church years later and found that the little lady had retained her healing. Hallelujah!

Incorrect View No. 2: God Does Not Necessarily Want to Heal You

At a meeting in San Diego, California, a woman approached me and said that she was experiencing pain in several areas of her body. I prayed for the first area, and the pain left. I prayed for the second area, and it was healed. Then I prayed for the final area. Nothing happened. I prayed again. Again, nothing happened. I asked a member of the healing team to take the woman aside to a private area for further prayer and ministry, during which the woman revealed her belief that Christians should always have pain, to remind them of what Jesus had suffered. It was something she had been taught in church, and it was blocking her faith for a complete healing.

My team member explained that she had been believing a lie, and then led her in a prayer to renounce that incorrect belief. Once these steps were completed, her remaining pain disappeared completely. She was totally healed, all because she had broken free from the trap of disbelief.

Incorrect View No. 3: God Sends Disease to "Instruct" You

The following testimony reinforces the fact that it is foolish to believe God "sends" sickness, disease, and other physical ailments for the purposes of instruction or spiritual growth.

> One of my friends was told about a woman who had been diagnosed with bilateral breast cancer and was scheduled to have a double mastectomy. My friend encouraged the woman to attend Joan's meeting, receive prayer, and cancel the upcoming surgery.
>
> The lady refused. She explained her reasoning this way: "God wants me to have this cancer. Through my suffering, God is teaching me how to defeat my pride."
>
> She had the mastectomy. Afterward, she realized she had learned nothing about pride. She fully regretted not having Joan pray for her.

Humility comes as a result of true repentance, not because you suffered a debilitating disease.

You do not need to suffer illness or disability in order to defeat pride and other vices of the heart. Humility comes as a result of true repentance, not because you suffered a debilitating disease.

Many people don't believe that God wants to heal, so they have little faith. Further on in James, we read this description of the attitude we should have when asking God for something, such as healing:

Let him ask in faith, with no doubting, for he who doubts is like a wave of the sea driven and tossed by the wind. For let not that man suppose that he will receive anything from the Lord; he is a double-minded man, unstable in all his ways. (James 1:6–8)

The *"double-minded man"* is he who prays to God for healing but wonders as to whether it is His will to heal. Again, the Bible leaves no room for doubt! If you need some reassurance, I invite you to revisit chapters two and three, which offer plenty of proof that Jesus desires to heal His children.

Where Is Your Faith?

Whether little or big, "storms" can produce the same effect in your own life. From a financial crisis to a physical ailment to a marital conflict, the storms of life can cause your faith to disappear, with the result that fear takes over, just as it did for the disciples in their sea-tossed ship.

Now it happened, on a certain day, that He got into a boat with His disciples. And He said to them, "Let us cross over to the other side of the lake." And they launched out. But as they sailed He fell asleep. And a windstorm came down on the lake, and they were filling with water, and were in jeopardy. And they came to Him and awoke Him, saying, "Master, Master, we are perishing!" Then He arose and rebuked the wind and the raging of the water. And they ceased, and there was a calm. But He said to them, "Where is your faith?"
(Luke 8:22–25; see also Mark 4:36–41; Matthew 8:23–27)

Notice what He said to them: *"Where is your faith?"* (Luke 8:25). Mark's gospel records Him as saying, *"Why are you so fearful? How is it that you have no faith?"* (Mark 5:40). The biggest sin in the world today is still doubt and unbelief, and it was that very same attitude that crept up in the disciples' hearts that day. However, while doubt and unbelief can keep you from receiving the miracles of God, in this particular instance, He still went ahead and completed the miracle—He calmed the sea and caused the storm to flee.

It doesn't make any difference what the storm is in your life; it doesn't make any difference what you're going through right now; Jesus is the One who can calm any storm. Put your faith and trust in Him. Don't let doubt and disbelief sneak in, regardless of your circumstances!

We are going to explore this topic further in the following chapter, focusing in on the fears that keep us from receiving from God.

11

CAST OFF FEAR

"I sought the LORD, and He heard me,
and delivered me from all my fears."
—Psalm 34:4

I t may sound strange, but there are plenty of people who cannot receive from God because they are afraid—afraid of the supernatural, afraid of Satan and his demons, or plain old fear of failure.

Fear of the Supernatural

Three of the gospels include the story of Jesus healing a man possessed by a "legion" of demons by sending those evil spirits into a herd of pigs, which then rushed violently down a slope, cast themselves into the sea, and drowned. (See Matthew 8:28–32; Mark 5:1–13; Luke 8:26–33.) When this event became public knowledge, the prevailing reaction was neither astonishment nor gratitude but fear. Take the pig farmers, for example—when they saw that the previously possessed man was now in his right mind, *"they were afraid"* (Mark 5:15; Luke 8:35). Pretty soon, the entire city was begging Jesus to depart from the region, *"for they were seized with great fear"* (Luke 8:37; see also Matthew 9:34; Mark 5:17).

Isn't it interesting that the people were not afraid of the demon-possessed man until he was clothed and in his right mind? Why are people afraid of the supernatural? The truth is, this kind of fear often prevents people from receiving the healing, blessing, or other miracle God has for them.

God is a supernatural Being. He is also your Father—and you are not to be afraid of Him! If you get your heart in a position of worship, you will find yourself receiving many more miracles. Pray to Him now, saying, "Jesus, I love You with all of my heart, and I believe that You will supernaturally bring to pass whatever it is that I need."

Fear of Satan and Demonic Spirits

The ninth chapter of Matthew includes a brief account of Jesus casting out a demon from a man who was previously mute, after which the man spoke, to the astonishment of the eyewitnesses. The Pharisees reacted by saying, *"He casts out demons by the ruler of the demons"* (Matthew 9:34). They basically accused Jesus of being in league with the devil. And the same thing happens today! The lies that were spoken about the ministry of Jesus are still in circulation. Don't pay any attention to religious spirits. Do what Jesus did. Simply cast out the devil and his demons!

Do not fear a demonic spirit. Recognize it for what it is and then deal with it, because Jesus gave you far more power than the devil has. His message in Luke 10:19 is for us, as well: *"Behold, I give you the authority to trample* on serpents and scorpions, and over all the power of the enemy, and nothing shall by any means hurt you."

He meant exactly what He said. Jesus transferred His authority to you and me so that we, too, could cast out demons. You can cast out the spirit of infirmity from another person and even yourself—simply speak the word and expect a healing to manifest.

When you are tempted to fall prey to the satanic whispers in your ear, ask yourself: Who has the ultimate answer? Who wins at the end of the Book? Recognize the voice in your ear. Does it line up with the Word of God? Or is it telling you lies? The enemy deceives with a lying tongue. Whom do you believe?

From the beginning, the devil was a murderer. He has never obeyed the truth. There is no truth in him. When he lies, he speaks his natural language. He does this because he is a liar. He is the father of lies.

(John 8:44 NIrv)

Who is stronger than the devil? Who defeated him at the cross? Are you filled with Jesus? Are you adopted into His family? Are you a child of God? If so, then you are greater than the enemy, and you have the power to stand against his lies.

Overcoming Fear

Have you noticed that whenever a miracle occurs, the devil is right there, ready to try to steal, kill, and destroy? (See John 10:10.) His deception will lead you down the wrong road—the road of destruction. Going down that road, your armor will fall to the ground piece by piece until you are vulnerable and open to sin which leads to the devil's playground.

Whenever the devil comes at you and tells you that your healing is not from God, you must stomp on him quickly and remind him whom you

Whenever the devil comes at you and tells you that your healing is not from God, you must stomp on him quickly and remind him whom you serve!

serve! Satan will trick you into giving up on your miracle unless you are wise to his tricks.

Why do you have to battle against Satan? In order to prove who you are, what you value, and whom you love—God. He created you for a divine relationship of love and worship to Him. But there is the element of free choice. He wants you to belong to Him, but He won't force you. He wants you to freely choose Him and His way. Only then can you show Him that you love Him, truly and unconditionally.

Put On the Armor of God

Jesus gives you the power to fight the enemy. How? First, put on His armor, which makes your mortal weaknesses invisible to the enemy. When you are dressed in the armor of God, all Satan sees is the size, the breadth, the strength, the power, and the majesty of your King. It is a very good idea to put on His armor every morning because the enemy can attack at any time.

> *Put on the whole armor of God, that you may be able to stand against the wiles of the devil....Therefore take up the whole armor of God, that you may be able to withstand in the evil day, and having done all, to stand. Stand therefore, having **girded your waist with truth**, having put on the **breastplate of righteousness**, and having **shod your feet with** the preparation of the **gospel of peace**; above all, taking the **shield of faith** with which you will be able to quench all the fiery darts of the wicked one. And take the **helmet of salvation**, and the **sword of the Spirit**, which is the word of God; praying always with all prayer and supplication in the Spirit, being watchful to this end with all perseverance and supplication for all the saints.*   (Ephesians 6:11, 13–18)

Remember, you have access to all Jesus' authority, and through Him, you have more power than the devil! *"He who is in you is greater than he who is in the world"* (1 John 4:4).

Stand On the Truth

If you know God's Word, you will recognize His voice when He speaks to you, in the same way that I always knew when my mom was calling me on the phone. She never needed to say, "Hi, Joan! It's Mom!" I just knew her voice. I could recognize it anytime, anywhere. I knew the inflections in her voice. Even when I read one of the books she authored, I can hear her voice through the printed words.

Your relationship with God is meant to be the same. To know Him well enough to recognize His voice, you have to spend time with Him, praying and reading His Word. As you develop a relationship of intimacy with your heavenly Father, you are instantly able to recognize the leading of the Holy Spirit when He guides you away from the temptations of the enemy. Fill yourself up with God's Word. Don't leave empty space for the devil to fill up with his lies. (See, for example, Ephesians 4:27.)

> *Then Jesus said to those Jews who believed Him, "If you abide in My word, you are My disciples indeed. And you shall know the truth, and the truth shall make you free."* (John 8:31–32)

Anything that does not exude the fruit of the Spirit or His gifts (see Galatians 5:22–23) is not of God. And everything that steals, kills, or destroys is from the devil.

> *The thief does not come except to steal, and to kill, and to destroy. I have come that they may have life, and that they may have it more abundantly.* (John 10:10)

We often hear the latter half of this Scripture being quoted, yet the first sentence is equally important. Anything destructive has its origins in the enemy. Yes, he is very clever, and he will sneak up on you when you least expect him. But you can learn to recognize his tactics, predict his attacks, and kick him out the door.

How can you tell? Line up what you hear in your spirit with the Word of God. You know the Bible teaches "Do not kill." If your mind is entertaining any thoughts that run contrary to that command of God, you can be sure the message

If your mind is entertaining any thoughts that run contrary to that command of God, you can be sure the message is not from Him.

is not from Him. If you suddenly feel like hurting someone, stealing something, speaking to someone in a derogatory manner, or committing another sinful act, it is because the enemy is whispering his temptations in your ear. His lies can be something as simple as "They shouldn't treat you like that. Get back at them. Don't ever talk to them again!"

Align Your Mind with the Word

How do you stop these negative messages? Line your thoughts up with the fruit of the Spirit. (See Galatians 5:22–23.) It is also very helpful to memorize verses that you can speak aloud in these circumstances.

> *Be anxious for nothing, but in everything by prayer and supplication, with thanksgiving, let your requests be made known to God; and the peace of God, which surpasses all understanding, will guard your hearts and minds through Christ Jesus. Finally, brethren, whatever things are true, whatever things are noble, whatever things are just, whatever things are pure, whatever things are lovely, whatever things are of good report, if there is any virtue and if there is anything praiseworthy—meditate on these things. The things which you learned and received and heard and saw in me, these do, and the God of peace will be with you.*
>
> (Philippians 4:6–9)

God says, "Forgive!" He also says, "Forget!" He may add on, "Fear not!" What would Jesus do in this situation? He is with you always, so go ahead and ask Him.

No doubt these experiences do test your faith. But unless you exercise your spiritual muscles, they will shrink and weaken, leaving you helpless. You would be no good to yourself or to others. As you learn to wear your armor and to build your spiritual muscles, you become equipped to teach others to do the same. The Christian army does not have to carry sharp spears, guns, or knives around to fight the enemy. We use the sword of the Spirit—the Word of God.

What else can you do? Prayer always comes in handy during a battle. Praying is just talking to God, so talk. The enemy doesn't want you talking to your Father and getting any advice, so speak and ask Him for guidance!

While you are praying, your mind gets so occupied with God that it cannot hear or concentrate on the lies of the enemy. Yes, prayer is a good weapon to use at all times.

Satan doesn't like to hear praise and worship directed toward the Father, either. Having good music available is not only soothing to your soul; it drives the enemy back to where he came from. He runs. Keep His music playing in your house 24/7. It is so easy today to do that with the Internet, TV, and radio, as well as CDs, mp3 players, and smart phones.

So, you see, Satan has a purpose in this world. You can use him, just like God does. When he rears his ugly head with his lies, you can start laughing! God wins! You win! You know the end of the book!

Remind the Devil of Your Healing

A sixty-year-old lady in a superstore was dragging her foot as she walked. Kelley prayed for her. She was healed. Awhile later, he saw her in another area of the store and she was again limping. He reminded her of her healing. He also explained to her that limping is a habit that sometimes needs to be consciously broken or stopped.

PART IV:

CONDITIONS
FOR MAINTAINING

12

WALK IN OBEDIENCE

"The LORD bestows favor and honor;
no good thing does he withhold from those whose walk is blameless."
—Psalm 84:11 (NIV)

D isobedience is one of the most common hindrances to answered
prayer and healing, and it's a surefire way to lose the miracles

and blessings you have received. Some may stop right here and say, "I don't want to hear about obedience again." However, if you are truly searching for the glorious strength of God in your life, you will come to Him as a child, listen to Him, and in faith do exactly what He says.

It's an age-old question: "Why did this happen to me?" Only God knows why things happen. You may understand that, yet you persist in searching for answers. And search you must. Where do you look? In His Word. I truly believe Christians today are often blinded by the lies of the devil in this very important area of their lives. If you want to have the scales drop off your eyes right now, continue reading with an open heart.

Let me say that my goal in this chapter is not to brow-beat you. I will acknowledge that, through the years, God has effectively worked through "hellfire and brimstone" evangelists to bring people into the church and back to God. While it is true that some people need to be "shocked" into repentance, the Christian's relationship with God is a far cry from that experience. God is entirely loving, merciful, and patient. And there are many people today who have become immune to threats and brow-beatings because of past experiences and who respond only to the presentation of Christ's tender love. Regardless of which approach speaks more to you, the truth is that God loves you and is ready to forgive. Keep that in mind as you read on.

Rules and Consequences

In every area of life, the saying is true: "For every action, there is a reaction." Whether it's at work, in the home, or in your spiritual life, there are rules to be followed, with corresponding blessings for obedience and consequences for disobedience.

Is disobedience a sin? Yes, it is. If you tell your child to complete a certain task, and he refuses; or if you forbid your child to perform a certain act, and he does it anyway, the outcome is the same: your child is in a state of disobedience and rebellion. He may not have committed a crime, per se; but, in God's eyes, it is sin. As a diligent parent, you then remove or withhold a privilege, because *"he who spares his rod hates his son, but he who loves him disciplines him promptly"* (Proverbs 13:24). Proper behavior reaps great rewards. Improper behavior invites punishment.

This is true in most areas of life. Obey the law, and you will live happily. Disobey the law, and you may be fined, imprisoned, or even executed, depending on the severity of your crime. There is always the good and bad, the positive and the negative, in every situation. Through experience and education, you learn how to live and do the right thing. Choices determine what you experience. Government makes laws, parents set rules, schools have course requirements, employers have job descriptions, and God has blessed you with His written Word. In each example, there is a pathway to success. Follow the rules and be successful; do it "your way" and crash into unpleasant circumstances.

God gave you that choice—choose to live in "the world," or choose to live in His world. Just as each country on earth has established laws its citizens must obey, each "world" has its laws and the consequences of breaking them. To receive the favor of your parents and the privileges it brings, you must abide by their prescribed guidelines. The same applies to your teachers at school, your fellow citizens in the community, your manager and colleagues at work, and even the people with whom you enjoy close friendship. Rules, whether explicit or implicit, guide your every interaction. Why should it be any different in your relationship with God?

Seeds of Rebellion

Human nature, however, is self-willed and rebellious. You don't want to abide by "suggestions," such as "Speed Limit 55," "Smoking cigarettes may be injurious to your health," or "Just say 'no' to drugs."

You generate all manner of excuses to justify your rebellious behavior. Driving over the speed limit "just feels good"; "I have to prove I'm macho"; "I'm late for an important appointment." Smoking cigarettes "relaxes me"; "All my friends smoke"; "I'll gain weight if I stop smoking, and my husband doesn't like fat women. I have to please him, don't I?" Smoking marijuana "gives me a much-needed release from everyday pressures"; "Drugs expand my mind."

At first, most forbidden enticements look good; you dismiss the possibility of their being dangerous or destructive. But then, on the day when you find yourself on trial for breaking the law, under the knife for the surgical

Some forms of pleasure are from the enemy, designed to draw you into his clutches. That's why you must ask God to change your perspective on what you consider pleasurable.

removal of a tumor in your lungs, or in the midst of treatment for withdrawal, you discover the inevitable consequences of your rebellion. As you realize the results of your choices, you cry out, "Why didn't someone tell me ahead of time?" Meanwhile, someone *did* tell you, time and again; the messages simply went unheard or ignored.

Some people believe that anything pleasurable cannot possibly be sin. Yet sin can be enjoyable. It can be fun. This category of "pleasure" may bring a form of peace; however, it is always short-lived. Those who indulge in sinful behaviors may be laughing now, but what you see is skin-deep and leads to destruction. Ultimately, deliberate sinners will forfeit their miracles.

Some forms of pleasure are from the enemy, designed to draw you into his clutches. That's why you must ask God to change your perspective on what you consider pleasurable. Psalm 37:4 (NIV) says, *"Delight yourself in the LORD and he will give you the desires of your heart."* When you make God your greatest delight, He fills your heart with a desire for the things He approves.

Obedience Requires Knowledge

My people are destroyed for lack of knowledge: because thou hast rejected knowledge, I will also reject thee, that thou shalt be no priest to me: seeing thou hast forgotten the law of thy God, I will also forget thy children.
(Hosea 4:6 KJV)

With only a little knowledge about cars, a person can get killed quickly. With a little knowledge about drugs, a person can die. With a little bit of God's Word, one can live in darkness all his days. The enemy would love to keep you ignorant of God's Word. He tries to tempt you, saying, "Don't bother reading the Old Testament. You are a child of God. In fact, the Ten

Commandments don't apply to you, either. You should just concentrate on the New Testament." The truth is, you need to study all of God's Word—not just John 3:16. And that includes the rules and regulations God has set in place.

Obey the Word of God

Sometimes it is the simple lack of knowledge of a situation that keeps you walking down the wrong road, right into destruction. Only by reading God's Word and soaking in biblically solid teachings, such as at a church where you are fed the truth of the Word of God, will you grow in knowledge and be strong enough to recognize the enemy when he sneaks in with his subtle lies and temptations, and keep him at bay.

Hosea 4:6 plainly states that anyone who rejects knowledge will be rejected by God and rendered incapable of serving Him. Not only that, but for those who forget His laws, He will forget their children. What a responsibility we have been given! I don't believe this verse refers only to biological children—I think it means spiritual children, as well. You have a God-given responsibility to share your knowledge of God with everyone, that they, too, may walk in God's perfect will and obey His directions.

Obey Divine Promptings

You read about the blessings, you claim the blessings, and you sing about the blessings—and then you go home and wonder why you are experiencing difficulties in some areas of your life. You read, you sing, you pray, you witness; but maybe you ignore God when He says, "Reach out to that couple. They need someone to show them My love and to share a positive word with them right now."

"But, God," you reply, "she's the head of the Sunday school, and he's the head intercessor of the church. Surely, they have it all together. They should be reaching out to me."

Most Christians understand blatant "sin," e.g., anything contrary to the Ten Commandments. But what about just "plain old" obedience to God's instructions, through the promptings of His Holy Spirit? This is something between just you and Him! No one else will ever know the secret communication shared between you and your heavenly Father. And if you fail to carry out the directions He gives—for example, to minister to someone's needs—it is sin, according to James 4:17: "*To him who knows to do good and does not do it, to him it is sin.*"

The apostle Paul wrote to Timothy on the same topic:

> *Timothy, my son, here are my instructions for you, based on the prophetic words spoken about you earlier. May they help you fight well in the Lord's battle. Cling to your faith in Christ, and keep your conscience clear. For some people have deliberately violated their consciences; as a result, their faith has been shipwrecked.* (1 Timothy 1:18–19 NLT)

"Child, do you see that man over there by the side of the road?" God quietly says. "He needs some food. Share some with him."

"But, God, he is so dirty. What would my friends say? I'll do it next time, when they aren't with me."

"Child, that little boy has a terminal illness," God says. "Lay hands on him and command the spirit of death to flee!"

"Me, Lord? I know that the Holy Ghost lives within me, but I couldn't possibly lay hands on him. Your power might not work through my lowly body. Then I would be rejected and ridiculed as a fraud. I will go get the pastor or the evangelist we heard last night. They have the gift of healing."

"Child, this person is anointed of Me. Funds are needed to send his ministry team to foreign lands to minister My Word to the lost and hungry. Empty your pocketbook into the offering. I am your Source. I will supply your every need, just as I supply the need for mission work around the world through others like you," prompts God.

"Oh, but the rent is due tomorrow!" you argue. "And the boys need new shoes for school, and my husband will be upset if I give up my lunch money for the week. I already tithed on my take-home pay."

God is not looking for excuses. He's looking for you to obey His instructions, which He often communicates in nothing more than a "*still small voice* [*"gentle whisper"* NIV]" (1 Kings 19:12).

If you haven't heard from God for a time, try to remember the last thing He prompted you to do. It could be that He is still patiently waiting for you to share His love with that cantankerous neighbor across the road, to lay hands on your mother-in-law for that crippling arthritis pain she has had for years, or give an extra offering toward repairing the crumbling steps of the church building.

The Relationship of Obedience and Grace

The laws of the land must be followed, or the corresponding penalty will apply. God's laws and commands are also to be followed; otherwise, His umbrella of protection is removed, leaving you vulnerable to the enemy and his attacks, whether lies, curses, sickness, or poverty.

> *God's laws and commands are also to be followed; otherwise, His umbrella of protection is removed, leaving you vulnerable to the enemy and his attacks, whether lies, curses, sickness, or poverty.*

If you disobey God, He still loves you, just as your earthly parents still love you in spite of your disobedience. However, every sin, whether blatant or covert, handcuffs the grace of God and prevents His angels from providing all that He wants to give you. The more you rebel, the more vulnerable you become. And while God will never let you out of His line of sight, just as parents allow their children to stray just so far before calling a halt, He will never violate your will. The choice is yours: obey His commandments and walk within the covering of His protection, or rebel against His Word and leave the security of His protection.

Obedience Exceeds Sacrifice

To obey is better than sacrifice, and to hearken than the fat of rams.
(1 Samuel 15:22)

You can pray for hours and hours, fast for days and days, but if you refuse to give food to the hungry when God directs, if you search for excuses instead of laying hands on a dying child at God's prompting, or if you continue to dabble in the occult in the name of "research" when God tells you to flee, should you really wonder why you suddenly find yourself in a desert? Should you wonder why God doesn't speak to you for days, perhaps months, at a time? Should you wonder why His blessings seem so short-lived?

Of course, the message of the gospel is one of God's love and healing power. Yet there comes a time in every Christian's life when he needs to understand the positive and negative boundaries of God. God can be lovingly patient with immature Christians as He forgives and forgives and forgives. But just like earthly parents expect a little more from their child every year of their growth, God also expects a little more from His kids as they grow in Him.

Yes, you are free from the curses. You don't have to make animal sacrifices to "cover" your transgressions. You don't have to pray for hours to "pay" for forgiveness. The transition from "guilty" to "not guilty" for the Christian believer is quite simple: Just ask. Sincerely repent of wrongdoing and ask for your Father's forgiveness. When you do, He will throw your sins into the farthest ocean, never to be remembered again. (See Micah 7:19; Jeremiah 31:34.)

Obedience Is Key to Christlike Character

If indeed your first goal as a Christian is to be more Christlike, aren't you supposed to follow after His example? Was He obedient to God? Oh, yes—He *"became obedient to the point of death, even the death of the cross"* (Philippians 2:8). If Christ had allowed even a spark of rebellion flare within Him that night in the garden of Gethsemane, where would you be today? The cross wouldn't mean a thing to you, and you would still be lost in sin.

Jesus gave His life for you. He was God's perfect Son. Food and drink were always provided for Him. He was protected from angry crowds when He spoke the truth. God's power flowed through Him when He laid hands on the sick. And God's same Spirit flowed through Him when He rose again from the dead. If you are to be truly like Christ, you must follow His example in everything, not just imitate select characteristics.

Disobedience Often Comes with Natural Consequences

Even though God promises to forgive our sins and forget them, there are natural consequences that often result from sinful behavior, in the same way that there are consequences if you defy the laws of nature that govern the physical workings of the earth. For instance, gravity keeps you anchored to the ground. If you disregard that law and jump off a high bridge, you are going to be injured or possibly die. If you eat the wrong foods, you can't blame God if you are overweight. If you know smoking is bad for you, don't blame God for your shortness of breath, your persistent cough, or the unpleasant odor of cigarette smoke that permeates your environment.

Let's say, hypothetically speaking, that you destroy something in a fit of anger. Forgiveness is not going to replace the damaged item. Or, consider the person who abused alcohol and illegal drugs for decades but is now clean and sober. God forgives him, yes, but the effects of his substance abuse may contribute to a host of lifelong health issues. Yes, God will even forgive a murderer, but He isn't going to intervene to prevent the penalty of life in prison.

Blessing or Curse: You Decide

The most famous passage of the Bible that catalogs the blessings of obedience and the curses of disobedience is Deuteronomy 28. These often neglected or avoided verses may explain why you are plagued with many circumstances. The basic theme underlying this entire chapter is one word: *obedience.* Obedience to God, your heavenly Father. His commandments are the best "advice" you could ever hope to receive; His ways are *"exceedingly abundantly above all that we ask or think"* (Ephesians 3:20). And still His children question His expectations and doubt His "ability" to guide them on a day-to-day basis.

You need to understand the whole truth, not just part of it. Read on and be set free. A friend of mine who had neglected to tithe

Obedience invites God's blessings and allows you to maintain them; disobedience costs you every blessing and leaves heartache in its place.

suffered many years from psoriasis, until she read the balance of Deuteronomy from verse 15 to verse 66. Having finally reached a full understanding of what God was saying, she acted upon that Word, and she was healed.

If you are not being "obedient" to God's voice, you have chosen to be subject to the curses found in Deuteronomy 28. Again, it is your choice. Which do you want? Obedience invites God's blessings and allows you to maintain them; disobedience costs you every blessing and leaves heartache in its place.

Rather than include the chapter in its entirety, I have presented you with a sample of verbatim curses of disobedience, and the corresponding alternatives—the blessings of obedience—which I have paraphrased in modern terms, to make them more relevant to your life.

Blessings	Curses
"Now it shall come to pass, *if you diligently obey* the voice of the LORD your God, to observe carefully all His commandments which I command you today..." (Deuteronomy 28:1):	"But it shall come to pass, *if you do not obey* the voice of the LORD your God, to observe carefully all His commandments and His statutes which I command you today, that all these curses will come upon you and overtake you..." (Deuteronomy 28:15):
All God's blessings will surround you. No matter where you go, you can't hide from Him. He will shower you with blessings, whether you are in a large city or out in the country.	"Cursed shall you be in the city, and cursed shall you be in the country" (verse 16).

Blessings	Curses
Blessings will follow you wherever you go. Everything you touch will prosper. You will have a long, healthy life because of your faithfulness to God.	"Cursed shall you be when you come in, and cursed shall you be when you go out. The LORD will send on you cursing, confusion, and rebuke in all that you set your hand to do, until you are destroyed and until you perish quickly, because of the wickedness of your doings in which you have forsaken Me" (verses 19–20).
You will be healthy and strong. The Lord will protect you from disease.	"The LORD will make the plague cling to you until He has consumed you from the land which you are going to possess. The LORD will strike you with consumption, with fever, with inflammation, with severe burning fever, with the sword, with scorching, and with mildew; they shall pursue you until you perish" (verses 21–22).
The Lord will fight your battles and give you the victory.	"The LORD will cause you to be defeated before your enemies; you shall go out one way against them and flee seven ways before them; and you shall become troublesome to all the kingdoms of the earth" (verse 25).

Blessings	Curses
You will be mentally stable and strong. You will accomplish great things. You will see clearly.	"The LORD will strike you with madness and blindness and confusion of heart. And you shall grope at noonday, as a blind man gropes in darkness; you shall not prosper in your ways; you shall be only oppressed and plundered continually, and no one shall save you" (verses 28–29).
You will have a beautiful spouse and home to enjoy. You will have delicious food and meat to nourish you and your family.	"You shall betroth a wife, but another man shall lie with her; you shall build a house, but you shall not dwell in it; you shall plant a vineyard, but shall not gather its grapes. Your ox shall be slaughtered before your eyes, but you shall not eat of it; your donkey shall be violently taken away from before you, and shall not be restored to you; your sheep shall be given to your enemies, and you shall have no one to rescue them" (verses 30–31).
You will be surrounded by and enjoy your children and grandchildren. You will be strong and healthy from eating what your land produces.	"Your sons and your daughters shall be given to another people, and your eyes shall look and fail with longing for them all day long; and there shall be no strength in your hand. A nation whom you have not known shall eat the fruit of your land and the produce of your labor, and you shall be only oppressed and crushed continually" (verses 32–33).

Blessings	Curses
You will be a leader of men. You will lend to those who need assistance.	*"The alien who is among you shall rise higher and higher above you, and you shall come down lower and lower. He shall lend to you, but you shall not lend to him; he shall be the head, and you shall be the tail"* (verses 43–44).
The blessings of God will surround you and your family and be a sign to the world forever that you belong to God and have been obedient to His voice.	*"Moreover all these curses shall come upon you and pursue and overtake you, until you are destroyed, because you did not obey the voice of the LORD your God, to keep His commandments and His statutes which He commanded you. And they shall be upon you for a sign and a wonder, and on your descendants forever"* (verses 45–46).

Make Your Choice

Most people don't like reading the "curse verses" from Deuteronomy. No one wants to experience any part of them. All those things are from the enemy, but if you reject God's ways and His will, you waive your right to His protection, thereby opening yourself up to any combination of these curses. In my years of ministry, I have met a few people who appear to have suffered most of these curses. I can't imagine the difficult lives they have lived.

Everyone needs to know both sides of the coin—the blessings of obedience and the consequences of disobedience. It's your choice. The Bible says, *"Choose you this day whom ye will serve"* (Joshua 24:15 KJV). God gave you the right to choose the blessings or the curses. Which do you want to receive?

I don't think anyone would knowingly choose curses. He might be lacking education, in bondage, or blinded by the lies of the enemy. Often, listening to the world's view of life is the same thing as listening to the enemy, because he weaves his deceptions and lies into the fabric of our culture and society. He has infiltrated the government and our schools, effecting the removal of God and prayer from most of them.

Choose to Grow

As Christians mature in their walk, they should become increasingly sensitive to God's voice and the promptings of His Holy Spirit. Heeding God's guidance will keep you following the right path and will help you to avoid any problems ahead.

Choose to Repent

If your conscience is bothered by something you have done, accept the warning sign. Repent and ask God's forgiveness. Don't gamble with "getting by" with anything. God knows what you have done, when you did it, and why. And He won't forget it until you've repented and asked for His forgiveness.

His promises are true and last forever. No one has to beg, plead, weep, or wail to get His attention. He even says to "remind" Him of His Word. He hasn't forgotten His promises to you; however, He does want to know that you recognize your rights as one of His kids and can exercise your faith in His Word, His covenant.

God made a covenant with Abraham long ago to bless his descendants forever. A covenant is a promise, a contract between two entities. God's covenant promise is still in effect. He hasn't canceled it. To access that covenant, all you must do is love Him and keep His commandments.

Blessings That Endure

*Therefore know that the LORD your God, He is God, the faithful God who **keeps covenant and mercy for a thousand generations** with those who love Him and keep His commandments....Then it shall come to* *pass, because you listen to these judgments, and keep and do them, that the* LORD *your God will keep with you the covenant and the mercy which He swore to your fathers. And He will love you and bless you and multiply you....* (Deuteronomy 7:9, 12)

According to this passage, your reaction to God determines His reaction to your children. Your disobedience will not just affect your life; it will carry on through generations. God says, *"I lay the sins of the parents upon their children; the entire family is affected—even children in the third and fourth generations of those who reject me"* (Exodus 20:5 NLT). He said the same thing in Exodus 34:7, Numbers 14:18, and Deuteronomy 5:9.

But the blessings of your obedience also endure. God also says, *"I lavish unfailing love to a thousand generations. I forgive iniquity, rebellion, and sin"* (Exodus 34:7). You may or may not have material things to leave as an inheritance to your children and grandchildren, but which is more important: money or God's eternal blessings?

The point is, obedience to God reaps great blessings in your life, as well as creates a legacy of blessing to be passed down through future generations. When you accept God's ways and live a life pleasing to Him, you keep His miracles in your camp—and keep the curses of disobedience out of it.

13

EXTEND FORGIVENESS

"Forgive, and you will be forgiven."
—Luke 6:37

Someone once said that it takes twenty positive statements, such as compliments, to cancel out just one negative, derogatory word spoken to a person. Having been called "Dumb-dumb" for many years, I can tell you now—it took more than twenty positive words to erase that nickname from my heart and mind. It took God's eraser of love, put into action by the decision to forgive.

Commanded to Forgive

This principle is especially effective in combating unforgiveness, which produces harmful effects similar to illness in our hearts. It is amazing how fast negative, bitter, hateful thoughts can disappear when you start praying for the person who hurt you. You can't stay bitter and angry when you are praying God's blessings over that person's life.

To Forgive Is to Receive God's Miraculous Forgiveness

Forgiveness has been taught many times because it is so important in living the Christian life, as well as in receiving and maintaining the blessings of God. You can't say you are a Christian and make anyone else believe it unless you walk in the footsteps of Jesus. God doesn't walk in unforgiveness, so you can't, either. God forgets your previous mistakes and all of the times you have stumbled, so you have to extend the same "forgetfulness" to others.

> *For if ye forgive men their trespasses, your heavenly Father will also forgive you; but if ye forgive not men their trespasses, neither will your Father forgive your trespasses.* (Matthew 6:14–15 KJV)

The Message paraphrase of the Bible says it this way:

> *In prayer there is a connection between what God does and what you do. You can't get forgiveness from God, for instance, without also forgiving others. If you refuse to do your part, you cut yourself off from God's part.*

Miserable, unhappy people breed unforgiveness in their hearts, which eventually leads to bitterness, resentment, hate, anger, and many other attitudes that have no place in the life of a Christian. Without a heart change, often, the body and its diseases won't change, either.

To Forget Is to Maintain Your Freedom

[Jesus said,] *Come unto me, all ye that labor and are heavy laden, and I will give you rest. Take my yoke upon you, and learn of me; for I am meek and lowly in heart: and ye shall find rest unto your souls. For my yoke is easy, and my burden is light.* (Matthew 11:28–30 KJV)

God is telling you that His way is not only the right way; it's also the "easy way." Yet you may find yourself insisting on doing things your own way. Do you know more than He does? People who don't give their sickness to God have difficulty being healed. They are stubbornly grasping onto something that is causing the sickness in their body.

> *People who don't give their sickness to God have difficulty being healed. They are stubbornly grasping onto something that is causing the sickness in their body.*

What do I mean? For example, you know smoking is damaging your lungs and other areas of your body, but you insist on continuing a harmful habit. You want your healing, but you insist on hanging on to bitterness and resentment toward someone who hurt you twenty years ago. Your spouse cheated on you, and unforgiveness overtakes you every time you think about that period of your life.

If you come to me with a long list of problems you want to get rid of, such as lust, bitterness, resentment, hatred, anger, jealousy, self-pity, selfishness, or envy, I am happy to pray for you. However, I will also take that list and instruct you to leave it at the foot of the cross, never to pick it up again. You have to be willing to give up all that garbage—that "dirty laundry"—that has been destroying you, slowly but surely.

Bad attitudes show on your face, in the sound of your voice, the look in your eyes, and the stance that you take. Defensiveness, unfriendliness, and unrighteous anger are all characteristics of the enemy. Do you really want to face the world or your family like that? Would you approach or care for someone looking like what I just described? Not Godlike, that's for sure.

How can you ask for God's best if you aren't willing to give Him your best? In faith, give Him the garbage—your dirty laundry—and forget about it, trusting Him to deal with it. You won't recognize yourself in the mirror when He gets done with you!

Throw Off the Hindrance of Unforgiveness

How can you find rest for your soul when you have bitterness, hatred, and anger in your heart? You can't. Yet Jesus said His yoke was easy and His burden was light. When your spouse or your child does something wrong, it's easy to allow resentment to sneak into your heart. Unfortunately, resentment is like yeast. The more it sits, the bigger it gets. It doesn't take long to become totally out of control! Dirty laundry starts to smell before long.

My mother used to tell this story:

I remember when I was a little child, probably seven or eight years old, we went to my grandparents' farm for the summer. Grandma made some special homemade bread and put it in a little "warming" oven to rise. Then she and Grandpa left to pick peaches on a neighboring farm. When she left, she told us to be sure to watch the dough. When the dough rose one inch above the pan, we were to take it out and put it in the oven, so the bread would bake by the time they got home for lunch.

We decided to ride the plow horses instead! My uncle put the bridle on, and we were really having a wonderful time, when, suddenly, we saw the wagon coming up the road with Grandma and Grandpa in it, and we realized that the bread was still in the warming oven!

We jumped off our horses quickly; our young uncle, who was the same age as we were, ran the horses to the barn and then came running after us! When we got to the kitchen, I wish you could have seen that stove and warming oven! The dough was oozing all over the place, and we were supposed to be having it for lunch! It had run out of the warming oven, down the side of the oven, and over the floor, and it looked like a river of "goo"!

When I think about unforgiveness, I always remember the yeast bread dough that kept getting bigger and bigger until it got totally out of control.

Unforgiveness is exactly the same way. It starts off as such a minute little thing. If you allow it to fester in your mind, heart, and spirit, unforgiveness expands exponentially, until it takes over.

Forgiveness Frees You for Healing

When Jesus said, "*Come unto me, all you who labor and are heavy laden, and I will give you rest,*" I believe that He was referring not only to mental and emotional struggles but also to sickness.

A prime requisite for healing is to get rid of any bad attitudes. People with unforgiveness in their hearts are determined to have their own way. All the hindrances to receiving apply here. Pride and unforgiveness are strongholds that must be broken.

A good man out of the good treasure of the heart bringeth forth good things: and an evil man out of the evil treasure bringeth forth evil things.
(Matthew 12:35 KJV)

When evil things come out of a person's mouth, it is obvious that he has within his heart such attitudes as bitterness, hatred, anger, and resentment. Left unchecked, evil breeds evil, leading to death. The enemy's plans lead to death for every inch of a man, until body, soul, and spirit join him in hell, separated from God forever. Satan is determined to stop all praise, worship, and devotion to our Creator. He wants us destroyed and cast into the pit. Doesn't sound like fun to me!

Forgiveness Unites You with Christ

The greatest example of love and forgiveness is when Jesus hung on the cross. After the shame and torture Jesus went through when He was crucified, He forgave them! He didn't curse or condemn anybody, even though He could have. He didn't call down ten thousand warring angels who stood at attention watching God's Son be tortured and killed. Jesus could have destroyed those soldiers and religious leaders who condemned Him to death. But He held His peace and obeyed His Father's plans.

The story of Stephen in the book of Acts is another example of ultimate forgiveness.

> *And they stoned Stephen as he was calling on God and saying, "Lord Jesus, receive my spirit." Then he knelt down and cried out with a loud voice, "Lord, do not charge them with this sin."*   (Acts 7:59–60)

Stephen was saying, "I do not care what they did to me; I forgive them." If Stephen had not forgiven them, his story would never have appeared in the Word of God. I don't think anyone reading this book has gone through what Jesus or Stephen endured.

And yet Jesus forgave His disciples. He forgave the religious leaders who nailed Him on the cross. In fact, Jesus forgave you while you were still sinning. He actually forgave you before you even did anything that could possibly be called "sin."

Miracles Multiply in the Atmosphere of Forgiveness

> *If you find that your blessings are slipping away, make sure that you have not been harboring unforgiveness or another negative attitude that might block the provision of God or steal it away.*

Remember what Jesus said to His disciples in Matthew 6:15: *"If you do not forgive men their trespasses, neither will your Father forgive your trespasses."* That is a serious warning. But, oh, the blessings you receive when you forgive others! God forgives you, and the doors of heaven open to allow His blessings to pour down and overtake you.

This teaching is not meant to guilt-trip you but to get you to take a closer look at your life, specifically at your love walk. If you find that your blessings are slipping away, make sure that you have not been harboring unforgiveness or another negative attitude that might block the provision of God or steal it away. Ask the Holy Spirit to reveal anything in your heart that might be responsible for blocking your blessing. He knows the answer! Then, whatever He brings to mind, repent of it and watch as God fills your life to overflowing. When you have let go of unforgiveness, it frees up your hands to hold and hang on to His marvelous blessings!

14

GUARD YOUR GIFTS

"Hold fast what you have, that no one may take your crown."
—Revelation 3:11

Y ears ago, a friend was taken to a deliverance service. He was
prayed for and was touched by the power of God. As he lay on

the floor, God cleansed him from the cultic influences that had tormented him his entire life, and his entire countenance changed. Instead of darkness and concern, peace and light surrounded him. He later explained the experience to his wife, saying, "The people prayed for me, and I ended up on the floor." However, being "baby Christians" at the time, he and his wife did not fully understand what had happened—or, rather, what *hadn't* happened.

While the people who ministered to him had set him free from the demonic forces that had been tormenting him at the time, they never told him that he was saved and that he had Jesus living in his heart, to fight off any future attacks. Because of this neglect, they left him open to future attacks.

> *When an unclean spirit goes out of a man, he goes through dry places, seeking rest; and finding none, he says, "I will return to my house from which I came." And when he comes, he finds it swept and put in order. Then he goes and takes with him seven other spirits more wicked than himself, and they enter and dwell there; and the last state of that man is worse than the first.* (Luke 11:24–26)

The next year brought attack after attack. The enemy was very angry that he was losing a follower. There was no one nearby to guide this man and his wife into a shelter from the battle where they could learn their position in Christ. Six months and many tears later, this couple finally found the door to God's haven of rest, freedom, and refreshing.

In Spiritual Warfare, Knowledge Is Power

When a person is delivered or healed, he needs further teaching on how to maintain his deliverance or healing. Otherwise, his miracle may fade into the sunset, and the symptoms may return, sometimes worse than before. He may begin to doubt that God did anything in the first place; he may suspect that the person who ministered to him was not from God. Years later, he may say, "Oh, that Christianity. I tried it once. Didn't work!"

Grow in the Knowledge of God

In regard to ministering to others, be sure to encourage them to get involved in a good Bible-believing church where they will receive help in hanging on to their miracle and growing ever stronger in their faith. In your own life, be sure to guard the Word in your heart, and never listen to the lies of the enemy. Just like Jesus did, respond to the lies with the truth—the Word of God. (See Matthew 4:1–11; Luke 4:1–13.)

Why does God equip you? He has a job for you to do. He will always empower you to do what He wants you to do—His assignment. God sends teachers, preachers, pastors, and apostles to equip, teach, and empower other believers to help others, not just themselves.

Grow in the Knowledge of Your Inheritance in Christ Jesus

That the God of our Lord Jesus Christ, the Father of glory, may give to you the spirit of wisdom and revelation in the knowledge of Him, the eyes of your understanding being enlightened; that you may know what is the hope of His calling, what are the riches of the glory of His inheritance in the saints, and what is the exceeding greatness of His power toward us who believe, according to the working of His mighty power....

(Ephesians 1:17–19)

It is crucial that you know what the Word of God says in regard to your inheritance as a child of God. For example, it says in 1 Peter 2:24 that Jesus Christ *"bore our sins in His own body on the tree, that we, having died to sins, might live for righteousness; by* [His] *stripes* ***you were healed.****"* Did you catch the significance there? Jesus took your diseases upon Himself when He died on the cross (see Isaiah 53:5), and you *were* healed—past tense!

If you want to maintain the miracle of a healing, you must stand on the truth of Scripture. Don't let the enemy infiltrate your mind with his insidious lies: "You weren't really healed; that was just a fluke. You are going to die!" Knowing and quoting God's Words on healing, you can fight any signs and symptoms of infirmity, disease, or injury.

Similarly, when you know what the Word of God says regarding His promises to prosper you, you can fight the spirit of poverty and the mind-set

202 ⌢ *Miracle Maintenance*

of lack. If Satan tempts you to fear for your financial situation, you can proclaim Philippians 4:19: "*My God shall supply all* [my] *need according to His riches in glory by Christ Jesus.*" When you know what the Word of God says regarding His promise of salvation, then if Satan sneaks in and tempts you to doubt, you can stand on 1 Thessalonians 5:9: "*For God did not appoint* [me] *to wrath, but to obtain salvation through our Lord Jesus Christ, who died for us, that whether we wake or sleep, we should live together with Him.*"

The Holy Spirit: Your Guard 24/7

I have heard many people make comments such as these: "The Christian life is so hard. How can I possibly make so many changes?" "I am not good enough for God. I can never be like those church people. I will have to clean up my act before God will ever accept me." Many people go to church for a while and then "backslide." Back to church they go for a season, only to fall away again.

> *It is the job of the Holy Spirit to empower you to change as He cleans out the hidden places of your life, purifying your desires and making you more and more like Jesus.*

Fighting to "earn your way" or to "clean up your act" is impossible, in your own strength. Good news—you aren't expected to do these things in your own strength! It is the job of the Holy Spirit to empower you to change as He cleans out the hidden places of your life, purifying your desires and making you more and more like Jesus.

Of course, salvation is the most important thing. It seals your fate for all eternity. However, the process of sanctification—conforming to the image of Jesus—is a lifelong journey. Once you are saved, you have to learn to crawl, walk, jog, run, and finally soar among the eagles. The Christian life is not always sweet and lovely with no problems. We have already discussed the hindrances to receiving and the battle of maintaining gifts and blessings. The correct knowledge to stay victorious is necessary on a daily basis. The enemy is very crafty; he frequently comes up with a new battle plan. God's wisdom, granted through His Spirit, is critical to recognizing who, what, when, and how the enemy is planning to attack next. It is by His Spirit that you are most effective at guarding your gifts and maintaining your miracles.

> *And Peter answered them, Repent (change your views and purpose to accept the will of God in your inner selves instead of rejecting it) and be baptized, every one of you, in the name of Jesus Christ for the forgiveness of and release from your sins; and you shall receive the gift of the Holy Spirit.*
>
> (Acts 2:38 AMP)

Some people receive the Holy Spirit immediately upon accepting Christ. However, there are many people who have come to salvation but have never known the added benefit of the Holy Spirit. In your spiritual inheritance, the Holy Spirit is like the icing on the cake. Salvation is fantastic; a relationship with Jesus is fantastic; but the indwelling Holy Spirit takes the entire experience over the top.

Being saved without the Spirit's assistance to stay on the straight and narrow is difficult. But when you welcome the Holy Spirit into your heart, mind, and soul, He will act as your Advocate, your Counselor, your Mentor, and so much more. Words cannot express all He can and will be for you.

The following are just a few examples of how the Holy Spirit works on your behalf.

Assurance of Salvation

It is the Holy Spirit who testifies to our salvation. It says in Romans 8:16, "*The Spirit Himself bears witness with our spirit that we are children of God, and if children, then heirs; heirs of God and joint heirs with Christ.*" The Holy Spirit confirms to your heart that you are a child of God and therefore an heir of Christ—therefore, it is only in Him that you find the confidence to believe that you will receive the riches of your inheritance we were just talking about!

Intercession on Your Behalf

Along those lines, the Holy Spirit also intercedes on your behalf, praying when you can't find the words to say.

For we do not know what we should pray for as we ought, but the Spirit Himself makes intercession for us with groanings which cannot be uttered. Now He who searches the hearts knows what the mind of the Spirit is, because He makes intercession for the saints according to the will of God.

(Romans 8:26–27)

What a marvelous gift! When you don't know what you should pray for, the Holy Spirit steps in and does it for you.

Divine Direction

But the natural, nonspiritual man does not accept or welcome or admit into his heart the gifts and teachings and revelations of the Spirit of God, for they are folly (meaningless nonsense) to him; and he is incapable of knowing them [of progressively recognizing, understanding, and becoming better acquainted with them] because they are spiritually discerned and estimated and appreciated. (1 Corinthians 2:14 AMP)

We've discussed already how God, through His Holy Spirit, gives divine instructions to guide you where you should go, point out people to whom you should minister, and otherwise inspire your life. His revelations keep you vigilant of the enemy's schemes and thereby help you to safeguard the gifts he would try to steal from you.

Receiving the Baptism of the Holy Spirit

Do you need God's power today? Do you need God's power to receive God's best? Do you need God's power to maintain what He has given to you? Then seek, welcome, and accept His power in the Person of His Holy Spirit. This third part of the Trinity is vital to your spiritual existence and survival in the world today.

If you [really] love Me, you will keep (obey) My commands. And I will ask the Father, and He will give you another Comforter (Counselor, Helper, Intercessor, Advocate, Strengthener, and Standby), that He may remain with you forever—The Spirit of Truth, Whom the world cannot

*receive (welcome, take to its heart), because it does not see Him or know
and recognize Him. But you know and recognize Him, for He lives with
you [constantly] and will be in you.* (John 14:15–17 AMP)

How do you access this powerful entity of the Holy Spirit? How do you
plug into His power?

Ask

All you have to do is ask your heavenly Father for the baptism of the
Holy Spirit and be willing to receive the ultimate power that comes with
Him. Reach out to Him with your heart and receive! It is the ultimate act
of receiving that I know of, after receiving Jesus into your heart through
salvation.

If you are His child, having accepted Jesus Christ as Lord and Savior,
I invite you to take the next step and ask your heavenly Father to baptize
you with the Holy Spirit. Yes, you can ask a pastor or other believer for
prayer to receive Him. Someone may lay hands on you and pray for you
to receive; however, you can receive Him on your own, wherever you are
right now.

My dad, Charles Hunter, received the baptism in the Holy Spirit as
he was driving down a busy Houston freeway. I knew a lady who received
it while enjoying a bubble bath by candlelight. Thousands received
it whenever my dad and mom ministered to crowds around the world
during a healing meeting.

All you have to do is want Him to enter your life. He will help you with
necessary changes to make your life look more like Jesus'. He will empower
you to receive and maintain more than you ever thought possible.

Use Your Heavenly Prayer Language

*But you, dear friends, carefully build yourselves up in this most holy faith
by praying in the Holy Spirit, staying right at the center of God's love,
keeping your arms open and outstretched, ready for the mercy of our
Master, Jesus Christ. This is the unending life, the real life!*

(Jude 20–21 MSG)

One of the gifts of the Spirit is speaking in tongues—a language you have never learned to speak or understand. Many churches still hold this manifestation at arm's length with a frown on their faces. They question whether any part of the Spirit-filled life is for today's church, and they are particularly wary of the practice of speaking in tongues.

Yet speaking in tongues is just one aspect of the Spirit-filled experience, and it is a marvelous blessing. When you have no idea how to pray for a particular situation, speak in tongues. It is God's perfect language. You may not understand what you are saying, but God does.

When the situation you are facing has you up against a wall with nowhere to turn, pray in tongues. Just like regular praying, this means simply talking to God, except that you do it in a language He alone understands. If a friend is experiencing a major challenge, you don't need to know the details; just intercede for him or her in tongues, and God will know what your heart is saying.

Praying in tongues is a powerful gift which you have to receive when you welcome the Holy Spirit into your life. But it isn't going to pop out of your mouth unexpectedly. You have to open your mouth and allow the Holy Spirit to speak through you.

Discover Your Gifts

As we discussed in chapter two, when you receive the Holy Spirit, He imparts to you a special gifting.

There are diversities of gifts, but the same Spirit. There are differences of ministries, but the same Lord. And there are diversities of activities, but it is the same God who works all in all. But the manifestation of the Spirit is given to each one for the profit of all: for to one is given the word of wisdom through the Spirit, to another the word of knowledge through the same Spirit, to another faith by the same Spirit, to another gifts of healings by the same Spirit, to another the working of miracles, to another prophecy, to another discerning of spirits, to another different kinds of tongues, to another the interpretation of tongues. But one and the same Spirit works all these things, distributing to each one individually as He wills.

(1 Corinthians 12:4, 7–12)

Your intuition may intensify. Wisdom may surprise you at opportune moments. Witnessing may become second nature. Daily you may find yourself teaching or mentoring other believers, or praying for the sick with great results. The reason is that the Holy Spirit is working through you, manifesting His abilities.

Now to him who is able to do immeasurably more than all we ask or imagine, according to his power that is at work within us, to him be glory in the church and in Christ Jesus throughout all generations, for ever and ever! Amen. (Ephesians 3:20–21 NIV)

Often, the first part of this verse in Ephesians is quoted to support the ability of God to bless His children. Indeed, I quote it often. But right now, I want to emphasize the second part: *"according to his power that is at work within us."* There is no limit to what God can accomplish in and through your life if you surrender to His power—His Holy Spirit—at work within you.

Perhaps you need to return to the earlier chapters on receiving. Is your ability to receive being blocked or hindered because you are not allowing His power to do its perfect work inside your body, soul, and/or spirit?

Find Your Place in the Body

For by [means of the personal agency of] one [Holy] Spirit we were all, whether Jews or Greeks, slaves or free, baptized [and by baptism united together] into one body, and all made to drink of one [Holy] Spirit. For the body does not consist of one limb or organ but of many....God has so adjusted (mingled, harmonized, and subtly proportioned the parts of) the whole body, giving the greater honor and richer endowment to the inferior parts which lack [apparent importance], so that there should be no division or discord or lack of adaptation [of the parts of the body to each other], but the members all alike should have a mutual interest in and care for one another. And if one member suffers, all the parts [share] the suffering; if one member is honored, all the members [share in] the enjoyment of it. Now you [collectively] are Christ's body and [individually] you are members of it, each part severally and distinct [each with his own place and function].   (1 Corinthians 12:13–14, 24–27 AMP)

God's plan is marvelous. Every Christian is part of Christ's body on earth. We all fit together so perfectly to teach, mentor, and minister to one another. We encourage each other. We love each other. Even though we represent different parts of the body, we mourn as one; we rejoice and celebrate as one. Some Christians feel closer to their "brothers and sisters" in Christ than they do to their blood relatives. This is because the Holy Spirit connects them so perfectly.

As you encounter new people, you may find an almost instant connection with them. After a few of these experiences, you will recognize the "common denominator" in these relationships is the Holy Spirit.

Spirit can be known only by spirit—God's Spirit and our spirits in open communion. Spiritually alive, we have access to everything God's Spirit is doing, and can't be judged by unspiritual critics. Isaiah's question, "Is there anyone around who knows God's Spirit, anyone who knows what he is doing?" has been answered: Christ knows, and we have Christ's Spirit.

(1 Corinthians 2:15–16 MSG)

This spiritual connection is very pronounced when you gather with other believers at a meeting in a home or in a formal setting. You may hear someone say, "The anointing was so strong," or "The atmosphere was so peaceful." It is a precious thing to experience such God-ordained meetings with others who believe as you do.

In Matthew 18:20, Jesus said, "For where two or three are gathered together in My name, I am there in the midst of them." The more Spirit-filled believers who gather together in unity, the more powerful the anointing of the Spirit. Picture people scattered over a field, each one carrying a candle. Alone, the light is limited. Yet as they gather together in one place, the light shines bright and strong.

Is it any wonder that God's Spirit moves mightily in meetings of believers? The power intensifies until sickness and disease cannot stay. The demons have to leave because they can't stay in God's presence.

A Supreme Gift

Don't grieve God. Don't break his heart. His Holy Spirit, moving and breathing in you, is the most intimate part of your life, making you fit for himself. Don't take such a gift for granted. (Ephesians 4:30 MSG)

Your best safeguard against Satan's wiles—your surest way to hold on to God's best gifts—is to tap into the power made available by His Holy Spirit. Invite Him into your heart today!

Pray:

Father, I want everything You have available for me. I have invited Jesus to live within my heart and work through my hands, my mouth, my being. Now, I ask for Your precious Holy Spirit to also work through me. I need all the heavenly help I can get to fulfill Your will for my life. Bless me, Lord, right now, with all the gifts and fruit of Your Holy Spirit. Thank You, Jesus. Amen.

15

SHARE YOUR GIFTS AND GODLY TESTIMONY

*"Therefore take heed how you hear. For whoever has,
to him more will be given; and whoever does not have,
even what he seems to have will be taken from him."*
—Luke 8:18

*"Take heed what you hear. With the same measure you use,
it will be measured to you; and to you who hear, more will be given."*
—Mark 4:24

I God Gets His Blessings to Us

got divorced in 2000 and, in the process, lost everything. In the years that followed, I was forced to depend totally on God. And He provided for our every need—food, clothes, housing, college tuition, and a car for each of my four daughters and myself. Miracle after miracle kept us alive. We praised God every day. Did He personally deliver provisions to our doorstep? No, He used other people, including deliverymen and mailmen.

Because I lived it—because I have proved Him, day after day, year after year—I can share my story time and again. I can encourage you to do the same. All the glory goes to God, who never fails you or deserts you. I recognize that God is the Provider of everything I need. Remember, He may use other people to get the provision to you; however, He is still the ultimate Provider.

When you learn to watch and listen for opportunities to allow God's blessings to flow to you, He will bless your socks off!

Learning to Say "Thank You"

We talked about the importance of gratitude and praise, so I won't spend a lot of time on it here. But if you can't thank God from the heart for the small things and graciously receive His everyday blessings, returning praise and adoration of who He is, then how can you expect to receive your healing or other miracle from Him?

Learning to Acknowledge God in All Things

Many people mistakenly credit themselves with earning or obtaining certain things, such as professional success and personal wealth, forgetting that they are prospering only because God equipped them to do so. They ignore the Scripture that teaches us it is God who gives us the ability to get wealth—to make a living.

> *And you shall remember the* Lord *your God, for it is He who gives you power to get wealth, that He may establish His covenant which He swore to your fathers, as it is this day.* (Deuteronomy 8:18)

Read that verse again. Do you realize that in order to "get wealth," you need to be empowered by God to do so? He *swore to your fathers* by making a covenant with them; and to fulfill His promise, He is "obligated" to bless you, His child, with the ability and power to amass a fortune. He equips you with aptitudes, talents, strengths, wisdom, and abilities—some of which you have yet to even dream of using—in order to fulfill His plan for your life. You are but a small piece of the giant puzzle of life.

God doesn't lie, nor does He ever go back on His Word. He blesses His children, time after time. He even *delights in the prosperity of His servant* (Psalm 35:27 NASB). He takes *pleasure* in your prosperity, if you are His servant who advances His kingdom, pursues His goals, and proclaims His righteousness. But you need to acknowledge that He is the only reason you are able to "earn" wealth.

> God doesn't lie, nor does He ever go back on His Word. He blesses His children, time after time.

You need to give God all the glory and honor He deserves. He is the Giver of all good things. He gave you life. He has been next to you every minute of every day, waiting for you to turn to Him. He has led you through so much to bring you to this very important day in your life. He has fed you and clothed you. He has provided talents and wisdom for you to succeed in life, to His glory. Your family and friends, your home and car, every breath you take, every sip you drink, every bite you eat...all of it came from God.

You are the hands of God on this earth. Your hands are Jesus' hands as you touch others. With Jesus living in your heart, you should do what He would do in every situation. He gave you the option to choose.

God Gets His Blessings Through Us

I always say, "Be a river, not a reservoir." (On the sides of rivers are banks!) I also like to say, "If God can get it through you, He will get it to you!" Both are so true. God blesses you not only for your own benefit, but so that you may pass those blessings along to others. Once you have learned to receive from God and you have His blessings in your possession, you should ask

Him how He wants you to use those blessings. It may be that He wants you to simply be a channel—a go-between. It may be that the gift is not to meet your need but someone else's. God may have given it to you to share with someone in your life who needs that exact item.

The Blessing of Your Testimony

Through your testimony to God's faithfulness and divine provision, others will be set free from fear and will come to know the joy of trusting God to meet their needs.

Again, God doesn't give you gifts and healings and miracles just for your own benefit or personal enjoyment. You are not to hoard His treasures in a safe or bury them in the backyard. His goodness and grace are gifts to share with others. He has been faithful to you, and you are to be faithful in sharing His miracles with others—not only sharing them but sharing *about* them, in order to build up the faith of your brothers and sisters in Christ. Through your testimony to God's faithfulness and divine provision, others will be set free from fear and will come to know the joy of trusting God to meet their needs. What you do for others, God will do for you and yours. I live by that principle every day.

The Blessing of Your Time

When my mom and dad were terminally ill, I knew I couldn't ignore ministering to the sick and unsaved people around the world to sit at their bedside. Neither did they want to prevent me from spreading God's Word. Mom and Dad loved to hear about my travels and the miracles God had done at my meetings. They loved God with all their heart and knew I was doing what God wanted, not what I wanted.

God's orders superseded my wishes and those desires of my parents. They would have enjoyed my visiting every day, but their priorities were the same as mine.

These days, I block out special time with all my children. On those hundreds of days each year when I am away from my husband and children, I know that God is taking care of them, just as I knew He was sitting at the bedside of my parents while I was ministering healing and salvation to His children around the globe.

The Blessing of Your Talents

God freely gives, but His gifts have many purposes. Again, they are not designed to be hidden away. If you stay aware and alert in His world, you will meet someone or hear about someone who needs to see, receive, or hear exactly what God has placed within you. For instance, a lady in line at the grocery store is limping. You have the answer. Ask permission to pray for her. Allow God to move through you with the gift (knowledge) of healing. She gets healed and tells everyone she sees what God has done. Just like a pebble thrown into a pond, one seemingly small act ripples across a sea of humanity making a difference in countless lives.

Share your gifts—don't hoard them. If God has given you a voice to speak, speak! If He has blessed you with a great singing voice, sing! If you are a teacher, teach! If you have the gift of compassion, freely offer your shoulder to someone who is hurting. Share your gifts, giving all the glory to the One who gave those gifts to you in the first place.

His Holy Spirit is leading you today. That same Holy Spirit will guide you through the days to come. You have much to thank Him for—your past, and all the experiences that made you who you are today. Can you look back and reflect on the sometimes winding path He guided you through? Even those experiences you did not enjoy but somehow survived have molded you into a person God can use to help others.

The Blessing of Your Fruit

Abide in Me, and I in you. As the branch cannot bear fruit of itself, unless it abides in the vine, neither can you, unless you abide in Me. I am the vine, you are the branches. He who abides in Me, and I in him, bears much fruit; for without Me you can do nothing. If anyone does not abide in Me, he is cast out as a branch and is withered; and they gather them and throw them into the fire, and they are burned. If you abide in Me, and My words abide in you, you will ask what you desire, and it shall be

done for you. By this My Father is glorified, that you bear much fruit; so
you will be My disciples. (John 15:4–8)

This passage of Scripture is very plain. If you are a disciple of the Lord
Jesus Christ, you will be a witness to the world by the fruit that you bear.
What fruit, you ask? The fruit of the Spirit, which is *"love, joy, peace, long-*
suffering ["patience" NIV], *kindness, goodness, faithfulness, gentleness,* [and] *self-*
control" (Galatians 5:22–23).

Plan on being tested along the way. You will have many chances to prove
your position in Christ. When you prevail in situations that try your patience
and challenge your commitment to the Lord—when the Holy Spirit, whom
you "received," makes you able to react with poise and peace instead of anger
and frustration—you prove to the world the power of the One living inside
you.

Share Healing with Others

When God heals you and makes you whole again, you can look back and
talk about all the things He brought you through without feeling the pain
memories often can cause. It is almost like telling the story of another person
or watching a movie about someone else's life. It becomes your testimony
because you passed the test. You made it over the hurdles and stayed the
course. God has held your hand the entire time, and He will be by your side
as you progress into the next chapter.

Healed to Spread God's Name and Fame

Let's revisit one of my favorite stories of someone healed by Jesus—the
woman with the flow of blood for twelve years. (See Matthew 9:20–22; Mark
5:25–34; Luke 8:43–48.) I would like us to look at this account in greater
detail, drawing from two of the three Gospels in which it is related, because
there are some significant things this woman did before and after receiving
her healing that are instructive for us.

Now a certain woman had a flow of blood for twelve years, and had
suffered many things from many physicians. She had spent all that she

*had and was no better, but rather grew worse. When **she heard about Jesus**, she came behind Him in the crowd and **touched His garment**. For **she said**, "If only I may touch His clothes, I shall be made well." Immediately the fountain of her blood was dried up, and she felt in her body that she was healed of the affliction.* (Mark 5:25–29)

*And Jesus said, "Who touched Me?" When all denied it, Peter and those with him said, "Master, the multitudes throng and press You, and You say, 'Who touched Me?'" But Jesus said, "Somebody touched Me, for I perceived power going out from Me." Now when the woman saw that she was not hidden, she came trembling; and falling down before Him, **she declared to Him in the presence of all the people the reason she had touched Him and how she was healed immediately**. And He said to her, "Daughter, be of good cheer; your faith has made you well. Go in peace."* (Luke 8:45–48)

It is worth noting the five things this woman did:

1. She heard.

2. She spoke.

3. She acted.

4. She received.

5. She told others.

The minute you receive a legitimate healing, tell the world about it! That's what this woman did, and I believe that's why she received a total healing.

Healed to Heal

In those days, the multitude being very great and having nothing to eat, Jesus called His disciples to Him and said to them, "I have compassion on the multitude, because they have now continued with Me three days and have nothing to eat. And if I send them away hungry to their own houses, they will faint on the way; for some of them have come from afar." Then His disciples answered Him, "How can one satisfy these people with bread here in the wilderness?" He asked them, "How many loaves do you have?" And they said, "Seven." So He commanded the multitude to sit down on the ground. And He took the seven loaves and gave thanks, broke them and gave them to His disciples to set before them; and they set them before the multitude. They also had a few small fish; and having blessed them, He said to set them also before them. So they ate and were filled, and they took up seven large baskets of leftover fragments. Now those who had eaten were about four thousand.

(Mark 8:1–9)

In this account of Jesus feeding the four thousand, which is also related in Matthew 15:32–38, notice that it was not until Jesus gave away the provision He had that it was multiplied. And there was more food left over than He started with.

Here we have an illustration of how God works. When you "give away" healing by laying hands on the sick, it is amazing how the healings will multiply, affecting your own life, as well!

Publish His Praise

During the past many years, you have heard the lies that God is no longer on His throne; that He is dead. How can anyone believe God is not working in the world today, when miracles occur all around us on a daily basis? God uses miracles, such as instantaneous healings, to declare His power; to show the unbeliever that He is indeed alive and to remind the believer that He is nearby. His works declare that He is still very much alive and well on planet earth. Scripture says His works prove His presence. Your telling others about these good deeds makes His presence even more profound.

*Then we Your people, the sheep of Your pasture, will give You thanks forever; we will show forth and **publish Your praise from generation to generation**.* (Psalm 79:13 AMP)

Should you thank God just once for what He has done? No, you are to thank Him forever! He directs you to "publish" His praises for generations. Most people tend to think that "publish" simply means putting a book together. But the significance is much richer. *Merriam-Webster's 11ᵗʰ Collegiate Thesaurus* offers the following synonyms for *publish*: "declare," "advertise," "announce," "annunciate," "broadcast," "disseminate," "proclaim," and "promulgate," among others.

You aren't only to give praise to God, but you are to distribute and advertise, broadcast and proclaim, multiply and generate, create and parent praise, from generation to generation.

You aren't only to give praise to God, but you are to distribute and advertise, broadcast and proclaim, multiply and generate, create and parent praise, from generation to generation. When praise arises in your heart, you aren't to selfishly enjoy it. You are to spread it—to broadcast it—for years and years to come.

My parents started this process in our family. They traveled around the world broadcasting His Word. I have willingly picked up their God-given anointing and continue "publishing" what God has done and will do. I pray that my children will continue this process and pass it on to future generations.

Praise is for sharing with others. When you share His praise, you share His power. When you share your testimony, you are sharing His praises. You are spreading His hope, releasing His power, and multiplying His strength within another believer. Picture a large pond of water extending around you. As praise rises up within you, like that pebble hitting the quiet waters, you produce a ripple effect across the fields of time, affecting people for years to come.

Another word for *publishing* is *witnessing*. When you witness by sharing God's Word and offering your testimony, the miracles of God will speak to unbelievers, awakening them to the realization that what they have been searching for is Jesus!

All heaven will praise your great wonders, Lord; myriads of angels will praise you for your faithfulness. For who in all of heaven can compare with the Lord? What mightiest angel is anything like the Lord? The highest angelic powers stand in awe of God. He is far more awesome than all who surround his throne. (Psalm 89:5–7 NLT)

Even the heavens worship God for His miracles and wondrous deeds. The angels don't know sin, pain, or the healing power of the Father, and yet they praise Him continually. You should be praising God even more because you know the pain of sin contrasted with His mercy, grace, and healing power. You, who have been forgiven and brought into His glorious presence because He loves you, have so much more reason to sing His praises, don't you?

Proclaim to the world that God is truly still on the throne, and that He is the same yesterday, today, and forever! (See Hebrews 13:8.) Do you shout for joy and praise Him? If you do, He will take pleasure in you! Praise Him all the day long! Thank Him for everything, and keep on thanking Him.

16

PRIORITIZE THE PEACE OF GOD'S PRESENCE

"And the peace of God, which surpasses all understanding, will guard
your hearts and minds through Christ Jesus."
—Philippians 4:7

In our discussion of how to maintain the blessings we receive from God, it is important to acknowledge the one blessing that can never be taken from you, except by your own choice. I'm talking about the presence of God and the peace that it brings. He has promised His presence to all of His children, and it is your privilege to be able to count on Him to be with you, in the midst of joyful times and trials alike, whether you maintain your other miracles or not. The peace of God, which surpasses understanding, is a gift no one can take away from you. When you belong to God, who is the Author of peace (see 1 Corinthians 14:33), His presence is a guarantee that not even the devil himself can deny you.

Psalm 34:14 says, "*...seek peace and pursue it.*" While peace is certainly a gift from God, much of your experience of that peace hinges on your personal decisions. You must choose to align your life with the Word of God if you want to know the peace of God.

Life is made up of choices—get out of bed or keep sleeping. Eat now or eat later. Turn on the TV or listen to the radio. Watch the news or a blood-and-guts movie, which will upset you, or watch a funny movie, which will relax you. Allow the broken washing machine to ruin your attitude or reschedule your laundry for another day. Visit a loving friend or an irritable neighbor who always upsets you. So, you see, the decisions you make play a major role in the amount of peace you experience.

You do control a fair amount of the stimulation that is thrown at you during a usual day. But the peace of God allows you to keep your cool, in spite of every unavoidable battle you face.

> *Don't fret or worry. Instead of worrying, pray. Let petitions and praises shape your worries into prayers, letting God know your concerns. Before you know it, a sense of God's wholeness, everything coming together for good, will come and settle you down. It's wonderful what happens when Christ displaces worry at the center of your life.*
>
> (Philippians 4:6–7 MSG)

Ultimate Peace

Plenty of people pursue "peace," according to their own definition. Some claim to find peace in a quiet corner with a favorite book. Others find a peaceful state of mind by getting lost in the plot of a movie. Still others seek "peace" by drowning their sorrows in alcohol or using illegal drugs. Yet the peace that is found in these pursuits is temporary; it isn't lasting, nor does it truly satisfy. Everyone certainly has their own definition of the word *peace*. Not tangible or visible, peace is a state of mind which is longed for by the entire world.

Ultimate peace can come from only one Source—God! His Word says that *"the peace of God…surpasses all understanding"* (Philippians 4:7). In the same verse, we know that His peace will guard our hearts and minds in Christ Jesus. This supernatural state of being is almost dreamlike in quality. And to the minds of the secular world, a person experiencing true peace will appear illogical, irrational, and perhaps out of touch with reality. They may be described as crazy, confused, in a "dream world," or in shock.

If you are obedient to Him, He equips you to handle what is around you. He is really the One in control, not you.

Many of those descriptions are exactly true. A truly peaceful person does not react to the pressures of the world with panic, hysteria, or erratic behavior. These peaceful souls have learned an important lesson in successful living. They listen, they consider the options available, and then they act—or choose not to.

During the day, those who dwell continually in God's presence can be at peace, with a sense of rightness, of being within God's perfect will, even in the middle of a traffic jam or on a crowded bus. If you are obedient to Him, He equips you to handle what is around you. He is really the One in control, not you. You almost become the observer as He works through you to accomplish His will.

Why are you cast down, O my soul? And why are you disquieted within me? Hope in God, for I shall yet praise Him for the help of His countenance. (Psalm 42:5)

What a nugget of truth is buried within that verse! Even though David was deeply troubled, he knew that his true Source of peace would not fail him. There was probably a battle raging around him; he probably knew that the odds were stacked against him; and yet he had the hope that comes from God's "*countenance*"—His very presence. Just seeing His face was enough for David. And it is enough for you, when you truly experience the peace of God's presence.

Dwelling in the Peace of God's Presence

When you became a Christian and surrendered your life to God, you didn't just give Him your toes or your hand; you didn't pledge all of yourself to Him between the hours of seven and ten o'clock every Sunday morning. No, you gave all of you—the entirety of your life—to the One who created the world. He is now in control. And staying in His presence is the best gift of all. You should dwell there continually. "Impossible," you say? No.

You don't walk in your strength but in God's. You don't have to depend on yourself any longer; you can rely totally on His wisdom and power from this day forward. As long as you are doing what He told you to do, He will equip you with whatever you need to accomplish the task. You will be prepared, no matter where you find yourself.

Satan loves it when the children of God get upset, develop ulcers, and fight among themselves when the pressures increase. By doing the opposite of what the world expects, you throw the confusion right back in the enemy's camp. The Bible describes this strategy as follows: "*If your enemy is hungry, feed him; if he is thirsty, give him a drink; for in so doing you will heap coals of fire on his head*" (Romans 12:20).

The enemy will lie to you as long as you allow him to whisper in your ear, so just tell him to stop; he has to obey. True, he may need to be told many times, and he may come back disguised as some seemingly harmless statement or suggestion, designed to mislead you. That's why it's important to recognize his tactics—so that you can calmly continue walking in the peaceful presence of God. Ask Him for wisdom and discernment so that you won't get caught in the enemy's traps.

Pursue God's Presence

You can walk and talk with your heavenly Father all day, no matter where you are or what you are doing. At first, you may need to be intentional about spending time in the presence of God. For some, the first fifteen minutes of the morning may be ideal for making a focused connection with Him. For others, a lunch hour sitting quietly in the park may be the perfect time. Others may find that the quiet time just before bed fits their lifestyle. Everyone is different, so discover what works best for you.

You will soon find you look forward to this special time with your Father, whether you engage in heated prayer or simply sit with Him, basking in His presence. Eventually, you will find it easier and easier just to talk to Him wherever you happen to be. He is your Best Friend forever, and He loves you like no human ever will, with an unconditional love that allows you to fall down, scrape your knee, and run back to Him for consolation, peace, grace, healing, and wisdom, so that it won't happen again.

Create an Atmosphere for Praise

As you come into His presence, you may find that it helps to surround yourself with music that invites an atmosphere of praise and worship. So many musicians and singer-songwriters have heard the Father's heart and put His words into such wonderful songs to minister to His children.

As you grow in your Christian walk, certain songs will come to mean a great deal to you. When I hear the songs that are significant to me, tears well up in my eyes as I remember where I was the first time I heard them. Often, I needed an answer from God, and He spoke through the lyrics of a particular song to deliver the answer to my heart. Now the song simply reminds me of His goodness when He used the melody and words to talk to me.

The Perks of God's Presence

Do you want to maintain your miracles? Your healing? Stay in His presence and invite others to join you!

In His Presence Is Divine Direction

Daily seek more and more of His truth. He will guide and direct you always. Sometimes you get so busy that you don't take time to listen to His direction. You need to take special quiet time to be alone with God. And you should never presume to know what He is going to say. If He directs you to handle a situation one way today, He may change it tomorrow.

> *God is the Teacher, and we are His instruments. We are to obey, thanking and believing Him for the results.*

Sometimes, He directs us to minister healing for a certain disease in different ways. We don't question why we lay hands on this person's head, that person's ear, or the next person's feet to heal a problem in the back; we just do it. God is the Teacher, and we are His instruments. We are to obey, thanking and believing Him for the results.

You may find yourself ministering to a homeless man on the street or a crying mother in the elevator. When you communicate with God, it is a two-way conversation. You are thanking Him, while He is telling you what to do next. "Go around this corner, stop, and look at the trees for a moment, so the timing will be perfect as you 'bump' into the next person who needs ministry." That person may need a smile, a hug, a prayer, or the message of salvation. Listen for the divine promptings of your heavenly Father.

Remember, God is in control only as far as you allow Him to be. As soon as you attempt to take over the reins, God allows you to do just that. There's God's perfect will, and there is God's permissive will. He won't force you to follow His directions or to obey Him. You have to make that choice yourself. He won't box your ears to make you listen. His voice won't boom through the ceiling to get your attention. His still, small voice will prompt you to turn a corner down a strange street. Why? You may never know. He could be protecting you from an accident ahead. He could be directing you through a particular area of town because the people there need to experience the light that only a child of God can show forth.

God may direct you to pray for the people living in the green house on the corner or the little lady with her walker slowly inching down the sidewalk.

He may encourage you to tell someone at the grocery store, "God loves you." He may use you in countless ways, but you have to be receptive to His urgings, or He can't use you to do anything.

Someone in New York may be preparing to overdose on drugs. He needs God's intervention. He needs prayer. At three o'clock in the morning, most of us want to be sleeping. The next time you wake up in the middle of the night, instead of getting upset; ask God, "Does someone have a need? Do I need to pray for someone?"

Each time I awaken in the wee hours of the morning, prayer automatically comes to my lips, and soon I'm off to sleep again; I wake up the next morning totally rested. Of course, I didn't always follow this advice. I would wake up and fret and worry and work myself up into a state of total wakefulness. Getting back to sleep was impossible—and my entire day would suffer. I learned the hard way. Now, I just thank God for the privilege to pray for His children and start praying in tongues for whoever it is that needs that special touch, a special prayer. I don't know who or where or how. I don't need to know all the details. I just know that God is answering a prayer somewhere in His kingdom.

Listen to His urgings. Expect His direction. Learn to recognize His still, small voice as He guides your day. Release your concerns to Him. Allow Him to work in your life, even in the smallest details. He is faithful to perform His works in your life, if you allow His peace to direct you.

In His Presence Is Rest

He who dwells in the secret place of the Most High shall abide under the shadow of the Almighty. I will say of the LORD, "He is my refuge and my fortress; my God, in Him I will trust." (Psalm 91:1–2)

Rest in His peace. Curl up under the shadow of His wings. Climb into His lap and let Him rule your world. Remember the protective safety of your earthly father's arms? Your mother's lap? Well, God gives the same feeling. You don't have to seek Him out; He is with you all the time. Talk to Him like He is standing right beside you. In fact, Jesus lives inside you. You can hardly get any closer to Him. Talk to Him before you do anything and allow Him to tell you what to do next.

Psalm 4:8 says, "*I will both lie down in peace, and sleep; for You alone, O* LORD, *make me dwell in safety.*" If you don't feel His peace right now, ask Him to surround you with it, envelop you with it, and engulf you with Himself—the embodiment of true peace. Let His Holy Spirit minister to you as you dwell in the shadow of His wings.

In His Presence Is Security

Do you remember the first time you got lost or just couldn't find Mom and Dad when you needed them "right this minute"? Out of the protective realm of parents, a small child feels panic. As soon as the security of Mom or Dad is found, the child relaxes, peace returns, and happiness resumes. Just as a child feels protected and safe within a certain distance of Mom or Dad, you feel that same protection and safety when you are close to God. If you are too far away from your comfort zone, uneasiness creeps in. Go a little further and worry takes over. Continue in the wrong direction, and panic will control you.

How do you stop? Recognize what is happening. As soon as you feel the slightest bit of discomfort, turn around and run toward His throne room. Don't even try to do something on your own. Let go and let God. He is there, waiting to meet your needs, ready to keep you safe. He cares and will provide what is best for you.

In His Presence Is Power to Resist Temptation

During a particularly stressful period in her life, a friend of mine asked the usual question: "Why?" She was told, "Only God knows. However, what a witness you are to others. As you stand strong in faith that God is in control, their faith is increasing every day. You don't realize how many people are watching you. If you can maintain in the midst of your circumstances, they know God will help them make it through their problems, also."

When you dwell in the presence of God, He empowers you to do what would otherwise be impossible. When a crazy driver honks madly at you,

you can smile, choosing not to allow that behavior to upset you. When your boss is irritable and criticizes your work, you can choose not to retaliate, as you ask God to show you what you can do to make your workplace more pleasant. When the bills arrive, and your paycheck is late, you can choose not to panic and instead trust in God's provision. You can thank Him for supplying all your needs. When the doctor diagnoses you with a serious medical condition, instead of being consumed by fear, you can thank God for His healing power and entrust your well-being to Him.

> *When you dwell in the presence of God, He empowers you to do what would otherwise be impossible.*

In His Presence Is Protection

I will lift up my eyes to the hills—from whence comes my help? My help comes from the LORD, who made heaven and earth. He will not allow your foot to be moved; He who keeps you will not slumber. Behold, He who keeps Israel shall neither slumber nor sleep. The LORD is your keeper; the LORD is your shade at your right hand. The sun shall not strike you by day, nor the moon by night. The LORD shall preserve you from all evil; He shall preserve your soul. The LORD shall preserve your going out and your coming in from this time forth, and even forevermore. (Psalm 121)

Who else but God can offer complete protection in exchange for your total dependence on Him? He is always there waiting for you, ready to help you, deliver you, and heal you from this day and forever.

In His Presence Is Victory

But let all those who take refuge and put their trust in You rejoice; let them ever sing and shout for joy, because You make a covering over them and defend them; let those also who love Your name be joyful in You and be in high spirits. (Psalm 5:11 AMP)

God cares about even the littlest things that happen to you. He truly will give you victory in everything you do, down to each step you take.

God is your Deliverer and your Protection. Jesus defeated the enemy through His death and resurrection, and you now walk in the victory He secured on your behalf! Because of His victory, God is your Father, Jesus is your Brother, and the Holy Ghost is your Teacher. Who could possibly be more powerful? The outcome of the war has been decided. Although the battles with the enemy rage on, you know what the end result will be! Jesus is the ultimate Victor who will reign forever. And you will reign with Him, if you have become His child. (See 2 Timothy 12; Revelation 20:6.)

God cares about even the littlest things that happen to you. He truly will give you victory in everything you do, down to each step you take. He will be there to keep you safe from harm, as long as you are searching for Him and seeking to obey Him. If you are on the way to the corner to buy illegal drugs or are telling a lie, any harm that comes to you cannot be blamed on anyone but yourself. As long as you are following God's directions, He is faithful to perform His Word and give you true victory.

Your Eternal Reward

The best thing about God's presence is that you will get to experience it in all its fullness once you leave this earth and all its troubles and meet God face-to-face. "*We can see and understand only a little about God now, as if we were peering at his reflection in a poor mirror; but someday we are going to see him in his completeness, face to face*" (1 Corinthians 13:12 TLB).

Prayer

Join me in the following prayer for peace.

Father, I want Your peace. I long for Your peace. I don't want to control my life, Father. Obviously, I've already botched enough of my life. I always have to ask for Your forgiveness as I have taken over and tried to run the show.

Father, I give You control over the smallest thing in my life. Let me know instantly when I am not in Your perfect will. Only Your joy, Your happiness, Your peace can truly bring satisfaction and healing to my soul.

Father, guide my hands, my feet, my mind. Keep me in Your lap with my hand in Yours each day. Keep me under the shadow of Your wing, under the umbrella of Your ultimate protection, lest I wander away and get blinded and confused by the enemy's lies.

Father, keep me sensitive to Your voice alone. Let me always see You in all of Your creation. Remind me minute by minute that You are truly my Father, my Daddy, my Protector, and my Friend. Only in You can I have total peace. Only in You can I be strong, because in myself I am nothing but weak flesh, easily destroyed. But You and I, Father, are a majority. In You, I am victorious; on my own, I live in defeat. In You, Lord, is true life. Live through me, Lord. Let me hide myself in You. Let others see You in me. I love You, Lord. Let me always serve You and be a witness to Your ultimate Light of love, peace, and joy. In Jesus' name, amen.

CONCLUSION:

COUNTING ON VICTORY

"Everyone born of God overcomes the world. This is the victory that has overcome the world, even our faith."
—1 John 5:4 (NIV)

N o matter what happens—whether you're on a hilltop singing "Hallelujah" or in a valley of despair; whether you see miracle after miracle or find yourself still waiting in faith for one—you know that you will triumph in the end, because *"God...gives us the victory through our Lord Jesus Christ"* (1 Corinthians 15:57). Victory is really a choice you make and a way of life. You choose to walk in defeat or you choose to win life's battles. Why do I say that? Because God gives you choices all the time, and walking in victory is one of many choices He gives you every day.

When you choose to walk in victory, you are saying to the world, "I believe God is directing my path today. He promised to take care of me, and I believe exactly what His Word says. I am victorious! I am a winner! God and I together are a majority!"

If you are not walking in victory, examine your choices. Are you accepting defeat at every step? Are you carrying your burdens by yourself? Have you begun to doubt God's abilities to take care of you, your family, and your loved ones? Has your faith in your heavenly Father become clouded by the demands on your time? Are stacks of bills piling up around you? Are you suffering with a sickness you just can't seem to shake?

The enemy likes to distract you from what God wants you to do. When the enemy comes head-on with a disaster, such as a major illness, a car accident, or fire, it isn't too difficult to recognize his maneuvers and get your guard up. However, he isn't always that brazen. Almost more powerful are his subtle tactics of robbing you of time here and there with minute problems. Maybe his lies will come through a trusted friend. You misunderstand the message, and suddenly, seeds of division begin to grow between prayer partners. The power of agreement is diminished.

You can come up with dozens of "little" things that could develop into potential "irritations" during your day. But what you do with them is the important thing to consider. How can you make the right choices? How can you stay victorious? Do you have your arms open to receive His gifts, in whatever form they arrive? Are you following His guidelines for maintaining those gifts? Are you staying in the Word and in continual communication with Him?

Remember the discussion in chapter eight—if your mind is set on God and your mouth is praising Him, other thoughts can't enter. Yes, that's a good battle plan! When you are trusting fully in God, you won't be shaken, no matter what the devil tries to do to get you down.

No one knows the truth of this better than Jesus. Just when it seemed He was going down in defeat—after all, He was nailed to a cross and crucified—He resurrected from the dead and thereby dealt a final deathblow to Satan and his minions. He submitted Himself to a horrible death, all because He was pursuing His Father's agenda rather than His own. He told His disciples, *"For I have come down from heaven, not to do My own will, but the will of Him who sent Me"* (John 6:38).

To Jesus, victory consisted in doing the will of God, not in amassing wealth, achieving success, or even staying alive. If you want to be like Jesus, shouldn't that be your desire, as well? In the face of resentment, hatred, disbelief, and ridicule, Jesus followed His Father's will through the cross to ultimate victory. For Himself? No, for you and me. For our victory.

> *To Jesus, victory consisted in doing the will of God, not in amassing wealth, achieving success, or even staying alive.*

God is bigger and stronger than anything that may be hindering your progress toward receiving His blessings. Allow this revelation to move from head knowledge to heart knowledge, from little faith to big faith, from little strength to power. Trust Him! Let His Son enter your heart and live within you. Let His Holy Spirit infuse you with heavenly power, wisdom, and peace. Live by the gifts of the Spirit and the blessings listed in Deuteronomy 28:1–14. Read them daily to remind yourself of all the great things God has for you. And rest in the knowledge that, one day, you will no longer need to "work" to maintain your miracles, because you will be in the presence of your heavenly Father, where you will partake of His blessings for all of eternity.

Are you ready to be empowered to receive and maintain all of the miracles God has for you? If so, then pray this closing prayer with me:

Heavenly Father, my eyes have been opened to Your truth. I want and need all that You have prepared for me and my life. In order to fulfill and stay in Your perfect will for me, I give everything to You right now, today. I choose to listen to Your instructions and to obey Your Word as I walk within Your world.

Jesus, no man can understand the ultimate sacrifice You willingly made to open the door for man to join You in the Father's throne room. To honor Your sacrifice to save my soul and reconcile me to God, I freely welcome You and Your Spirit to work through me to reach others. Touch and heal through my hands. Speak through me. Use me in any way You desire. I choose to follow in Your footsteps.

Jesus, You are the ultimate Gift I need to receive from God. My part in this sacred covenant is to maintain my relationship with You by guarding my heart and mind, as well as equipping myself to fend off the enemy's advances. I thank You that Your Holy Spirit is always available to me.

God, You are such a marvelous, precious Father. Words cannot express the profound feelings of gratitude, love, and awe that well up within me when I praise You and simply bask in Your presence. You are my Source and Sustainer, and I welcome You into my life. Existence is nothing without You. I worship You with everything that is within me. In Jesus' name, amen.

ABOUT THE AUTHOR

At the tender age of twelve, Joan Hunter committed her life to Christ and began faithfully serving in ministry alongside her parents, Charles and Frances Hunter. Together, they traveled around the globe conducting Healing Explosions and Healing Schools.

Joan is an anointed healing evangelist, a dynamic teacher, and a bestselling author. She is the founder and president of Joan Hunter Ministries,

Hearts 4 Him, and 4 Corners Foundation, and she is also the president of Hunter Ministries. Joan's television appearances have been broadcast around the world on World Harvest Network, Inspiration Network, TBN, NRB Word Networks, Daystar, Faith TV, Cornerstone TV, The Church Channel, Total Christian Television, Christian Television Network, Watchmen Broadcasting, and God TV. Joan has also been the featured guest on many national television and radio shows, including Sid Roth's *It's Supernatural!*, *It's a New Day*, *The Miracle Channel*, *The Patricia King Show*, *Today with Marilyn and Sarah*, and many others.

Together, Joan and her powerful international healing ministry have conducted miracle services and healing schools throughout numerous countries in a world characterized by brokenness and pain. Having emerged victorious through tragic circumstances, impossible obstacles, and immeasurable devastation, Joan shares her personal message of hope and restoration to the brokenhearted, deliverance and freedom to the bound, and healing and wholeness to the diseased. Her vision is to see the body of Christ live in freedom, happiness, wholeness, and financial wellness.

Joan lives with her husband, Kelley Murrell, in Pinehurst, Texas. Together, they have eight children—four daughters and four sons—and five grandchildren.